F. W. Raiffeisen-Schule
Integrierte Gesamtschule
Martin-Luther-Str. 2
57577 HAMM/SIEG

D1703400

Orange **Line 4**
Standardaufgaben
Grundkurs und Erweiterungskurs

von
Bernadette Kesting

sowie
Pauline Ashworth

Ernst Klett Verlag
Stuttgart • Leipzig

Orange Line 4 Standardaufgaben Grundkurs und Erweiterungskurs

Autorinnen: Bernadette Kesting, Breitenworbis; Pauline Ashworth, Stuttgart

Zeichenerklärung:

⊚ Übungen mit diesem Symbol verweisen auf die CD zum Hörverstehen.

1. Auflage   1 ⁶ ⁵ ⁴ ³ ² | 2012 2011 2010

Alle Drucke dieser Auflage sind unverändert und können im Unterricht nebeneinander verwendet werden. Die letzte Zahl bezeichnet das Jahr des Druckes.

Das Werk und seine Teile sind urheberrechtlich geschützt. Das Gleiche gilt für Software sowie das Begleitmaterial. Jede Nutzung in anderen als den gesetzlich zugelassenen oder in den Lizenzbestimmungen (CD) genannten Fällen bedarf der vorherigen schriftlichen Einwilligung des Verlages. Hinweis § 52 a UrhG: Weder das Werk noch seine Teile dürfen ohne eine solche Einwilligung eingescannt und in ein Netzwerk eingestellt werden. Dies gilt auch für Intranets von Schulen und sonstigen Bildungseinrichtungen. Fotomechanische oder andere Wiedergabeverfahren nur mit Genehmigung des Verlages.
© und ℗ Ernst Klett Verlag GmbH, Stuttgart 2008.
Alle Rechte vorbehalten.
www.klett.de

Redaktion: Lektorat editoria, Cornelia Schaller, Fellbach
Satz und Gestaltung: Sabine Kittel
Umschlaggestaltung: Koma Amok, Stuttgart
Umschlagfoto: Getty Images (Clarissa Leahy/stone), München; Corbis (RF), Düsseldorf
Reproduktion: Meyle + Müller, Medien-Management, Pforzheim
Druck: Esser Druck GmbH, Bretten

Printed in Germany
978-3-12-547544-1

Audio-CD

Aufnahmeleitung: Ernst Klett Verlag GmbH, Stuttgart
Redaktion: Lektorat editoria, Cornelia Schaller, Fellbach
Aufgenommen in Q Sound, London
Aufnahme: Tim Woolf
Produktion: John Green, TEFL Tapes
Sprecherinnen und Sprecher: Sophie Aldred, Philippa Alexander, Laurence Bouvard, Brian Bowles, Nick Cass, John Chancer, Clare Corbett, DeNica Fairman, Roscoe Fenton, James Goode, Nigel Greaves, John Hasler, Harriet Kershaw, Lorelei King, Victoria Kruger, Walter Lewis, Alan Marriott, Rhonda Millar, Gina Murray, Christopher Ragland, Penny Rawlins, Bill Roberts, Martin T. Sherman, Rhys Swinburn, Myles Taylor, Mille Upton, Leah White, Jennifer Woodward
Tontechnik: Tim Woolf
Presswerk: Optimal Media Production GmbH, Röbel/Müritz

Gesamtzeit: 51'41"

Inhalt

Die Lösungen mit HV-Texten sowie zusätzliche HV- und LV-Texte
finden Sie auf der hinten eingeklebten Lehrersoftware-CD.

Unit 1   I ♥ New York City

🔊 1 Let's listen: What's for lunch?

GK a) *Right or wrong? Tick (✔) the right box.*

	right	wrong	not in the text
1. Jenna had breakfast an hour ago.			
2. Matt ate two bagels and a pancake for lunch.			
3. Matt wants to have a second breakfast.			
4. It's 11:30.			

EK a) *Who of them did it? Tick (✔) the right person.*

Who …	Matt	Jenna	Matt's mum
1. only had breakfast an hour ago?			
2. had jogged before breakfast?			
3. had heard a noise at the door?			
4. had gone to work at 5 o'clock?			
5. had brought fresh bagels?			
6. ate three bagels and a pancake?			

EK b) *Tick (✔) the right box.*

1. Jenna hates cream cheese. ☐
2. Jenna hates eggs. ☐
3. Jenna hates bacon. ☐

GK b) *What does Jenna think and feel? Tick (✔) the right box.*

1. She can understand that Matt is very hungry. ☐
2. She feels sorry for Matt because he is so tired. ☐
3. She is surprised that Matt is hungry again. ☐

GK + EK c) *What do Matt and Jenna have for lunch? Write down the right letter for each of them.*

Matt has _____.   Jenna has _____.

A) 🍴 pancakes with maple syrup
🍴 bagels
☺ coffee

B) 🍴 a sandwich with egg, bacon and turkey
🍴 French fries
☺ coffee

C) 🍴 a sandwich with ham, cheese, turkey, tomato and lettuce
☺ a strawberry milkshake

D) 🍴 a sandwich with bacon, cheese, turkey, tomato and lettuce
☺ a strawberry milkshake

E) 🍴 a sandwich with bacon, cheese, turkey, tomato and lettuce
☺ coffee

F) 🍴 a sandwich with cream cheese, bacon and turkey
🍴 French fries
☺ coffee

GK + EK d) *How much? Write down the numbers.*

Matt's and Jenna's lunch is $ _____. Jenna gives the waiter $ _____.

Orange Line 4
ISBN 978-3-12-547544-1

© Ernst Klett Verlag GmbH, Stuttgart 2008 | www.klett.de
Von dieser Druckvorlage ist die Vervielfältigung für den eigenen Unterrichtsgebrauch
gestattet. Die Kopiergebühren sind abgegolten. Alle Rechte vorbehalten.

Klett

2 Let's read: The Empire State Building

GK + EK In the 1920's and 1930's everybody wanted to have the world's highest building. That is why John J. Raskob gave the money to build the Empire State Building in 1930.

They started to build on 17th March 1930 and they finished 410 days later, on 1st May 1931. It has 102 floors[1] and is 381 meters high. With the television tower on top, it is almost 449 meters high. Over 3,400 people worked on the building and most of them were from Europe or were Mohawks, who are Native Americans. They needed people who were not scared of heights and they found them. There are many photographs which show workers who had their lunch hundreds of meters above the ground with nothing to protect them. Official[2] numbers show that only 14 people died because they fell.

Before they finished the Empire State Building, the Chrysler Building had been the tallest building in the world and then the Bank of Manhattan at 40 Wall Street was the tallest. They had kept their titles only for a year because people with money planned every new building higher and higher. It was like a race to the clouds. The Empire State Building was the winner of the race – it stayed the world's tallest skyscraper for over 40 years. The building got its name because the State of New York is also called the 'Empire State'.

EK The Empire State Building is at the corner of 5th Avenue and 34th Street and they built it in the place where the Waldorf-Astoria Hotel had once been. The hotel was also very famous because at the end of the 19th century the rich and beautiful people of New York had often stayed or eaten there. This group of people were called *The Four Hundred* and they were the people you had to know if you wanted to be somebody in New York at the time. Today the Waldorf-Astoria is at 301, Park Avenue. Many people have died in or around the building but some people have also been very lucky. In 1945, on Saturday, 28th July, a plane flew into the building. It was an accident and it happened because it was a very foggy day. Fourteen people died but one woman was very lucky. Betty Lou Oliver was in an elevator[3] when it fell 75 floors down but she lived. The building opened again for work on the Monday, only two days later. In 1979 another woman was very lucky. Elvita Adams fell from the 86th floor but the wind blew her back into the 85th floor and she only broke her hip[4].

K + EK You can visit the Empire State Building and have a great view of New York or you can just look at the building from outside. Even at night you can always see the building because there are beautiful lights at the top. They also change color at different times of the year. On 4th July they are red, white and blue. At Christmas they are red and green and when the Yankees play at home, they become blue and white. For Christopher Street Day they go pink.

[1]floor [flɔː] – *Stockwerk,* [2]official [əˈfɪʃəl] – *offiziell/veröffentlicht,* [3]elevator [ˈelɪveɪtə] – *Aufzug,* [4]hip [hɪp] – *Hüfte*

Read the text and complete the fact box.

K + EK

◎ ◎ **FACT BOX** ◎ ◎

Building time:
➲ started: _____/finished: _____

Size/height:
➲ how high: _____ (with TV tower: _____)

➲ number of floors: _____

Other buildings that fought for the title of highest building:

➲ 1) _____/2) _____

➲ how long the ESB could keep the title: _____

 © Ernst Klett Verlag GmbH, Stuttgart 2008 | www.klett.de
Von dieser Druckvorlage ist die Vervielfältigung für den eigenen Unterrichtsgebrauch gestattet. Die Kopiergebühren sind abgegolten. Alle Rechte vorbehalten.

Orange Line 4
ISBN 978-3-12-547544-1

People who worked on it:

➲ number: _____

➲ where from/who

• _____

• _____

➲ qualification for the job: _____

Official number of people who died while working on the ESB:

_____

Lights at night:

➲ on 4th July: _____

➲ at Christmas: _____

➲ when Yankees play at home: _____

➲ on Christopher Street Day: _____

EK

◉◎ MORE INTERESTING FACTS ◎◉

Place:

➲ where: _____

➲ what had been there before: _____

➲ famous because _____

EK

◉◎ LUCKY WOMEN ◎◉

Woman 1:	**Woman 2:**
➲ who: _____	➲ who: _____
➲ when: _____	➲ when: _____
➲ what: _____	➲ what: _____
➲ why: _____	_____
➲ how many died: _____	➲ why she was lucky: _____
➲ why she was lucky: _____	_____
_____	_____
_____	_____
_____	_____

Orange Line 4
ISBN 978-3-12-547544-1

© Ernst Klett Verlag GmbH, Stuttgart 2008 | www.klett.de
Von dieser Druckvorlage ist die Vervielfältigung für den eigenen Unterrichtsgebrauch
gestattet. Die Kopiergebühren sind abgegolten. Alle Rechte vorbehalten.

GK **3 The Mayflower**

Fill in the verbs in the simple past.

Have you ever heard of the Mayflower? She was one of the first ships that __took__ *(to take*)*

a group of people from Europe to the New World.

On 6th September, 1620 the Mayflower _____ *(to leave*)* Plymouth in England for a

journey that _____ *(to make*)* history. The 102 passengers on the ship _____

(to hope) to start a new and better life in America.

The first part of their journey across the Atlantic Ocean was OK. But their luck _____

(to change) half way to America when bad storms _____ *(to start)* to hit the Mayflower.

The passengers _____ *(to have*)* to stay below deck and _____ *(to feel*)* cold, wet

and seasick. During one of the storms Elizabeth Hopkins _____ *(to give*)* birth to a boy.

She _____ *(to name)* her son Oceanus. On 11th November, after two months on the

Atlantic Ocean, they finally _____ *(to see*)* land.   *irregular verb

EK Have you ever heard of the Mayflower? She was one of the first ships that _____ *(to take)*

a group of people from Europe to the New World.

On 6th September, 1620 the Mayflower _____ *(to leave)* Plymouth in England for a journey

that _____ *(to make)* history. There _____ *(to be)* 102 passengers on the ship who

_____ *(to hope)* to start a new and better life in America.

The first part of their journey across the Atlantic Ocean _____ *(to be)* OK. The wind and

weather _____ *(to be)* good for sailing and only some of the passengers _____

(to be) seasick. But their luck _____ *(to change)* half way to America when bad storms

_____ *(to begin)* to hit the Mayflower. The passengers _____ *(to have)* to stay

below deck and _____ *(to be)* cold, wet and seasick. During one of the storms Elizabeth

Hopkins _____ *(to give)* birth to a boy. She _____ *(to name)* her son Oceanus.

On 11th November, after two months on the Atlantic Ocean, they finally _____ *(to see)*

land.

 © Ernst Klett Verlag GmbH, Stuttgart 2008 | www.klett.de
Von dieser Druckvorlage ist die Vervielfältigung für den eigenen Unterrichtsgebrauch
gestattet. Die Kopiergebühren sind abgegolten. Alle Rechte vorbehalten.

Orange Line 4
ISBN 978-3-12-547544-1

4 A journey across the ocean in those days

GK *Write five sentences. Use the negative form in the simple past. Look at the example.*

1. in those days ships – not have rooms for the passengers	2. the passengers – not sleep in beds, but on the floor on or below deck	3. the ships – not have bathrooms or toilets
4. the passengers – not eat their meals in a dining room, but on deck	5. during their journey they – not get fresh fruit or vegetables	6. in those days most people – not know how to swim and died when they fell into the sea

1. ___In those days ships didn't have rooms for the passengers.___

2. _____

3. _____

4. _____

5. _____

6. _____

EK *Write five sentences in the simple past. Some are positive and some are negative.*
Find the right conjunction between parts a) and b). Look at the example and finish it.

1. a) in the 17th century a journey across the ocean – not easy b) in those days ships – not have rooms for the passengers		2. a) life on a ship – not comfortable b) the passengers – not sleep in beds, but on the floor on or below deck
3. a) the ships – not have bathrooms or toilets b) the journey – take a few weeks	4. a) after some weeks – there often not enough food and fresh water for all the people b) many people – became sick	5. a) in those days most people – not know how to swim b) many – die when they fell into the sea

1. ___In the 17th century a journey across the ocean wasn't easy because in those days___

_____

2. _____

_____

3. _____

_____

4. _____

_____

5. _____

_____

Orange Line 4
ISBN 978-3-12-547544-1

© Ernst Klett Verlag GmbH, Stuttgart 2008 | www.klett.de
Von dieser Druckvorlage ist die Vervielfältigung für den eigenen Unterrichtsgebrauch
gestattet. Die Kopiergebühren sind abgegolten. Alle Rechte vorbehalten.

Klett

5 Questions to a 17th century passenger

Imagine you could ask someone who lived in the 17th century about a journey to America.

GK a) *Put the words into the right order and make questions.*

1. many bad storms • did • have • during your journey • you
2. did • enough to eat • have • you
3. did • enough • fresh water • take • for all the passengers • they
4. did • on or below deck • sleep • you

EK a) *Make questions with 'Did ...?' or 'Was/Were ...?'.*

1. you have many bad storms during your journey
2. you often seasick
3. you have enough to eat
4. there enough fresh water for all the passengers
5. you sleep on or below deck

_____

_____

_____

_____

_____

_____

b) *Ask five questions in the simple past. Use a question word. Look at the example.*

GK

 How / How often / What / When / Where / Why / ...
+ 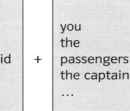 did
+  you / the / passengers / the captain / ...
+ 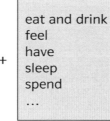 eat and drink / feel / have / sleep / spend / ...
+  ... ?

EK

How / How (big/fast/bad/...) / How (long/often/many/...) / What / When / Where / Why / ...
+ ...
+ the weather / the ship / the storms / the journey / you / the / passengers / the captain / ...
+ eat and drink / have / sleep / feel / ...
+ ... ?

<u>How often did you have bad storms?</u>

_____

_____

_____

_____

© Ernst Klett Verlag GmbH, Stuttgart 2008 | www.klett.de
Von dieser Druckvorlage ist die Vervielfältigung für den eigenen Unterrichtsgebrauch gestattet. Die Kopiergebühren sind abgegolten. Alle Rechte vorbehalten.

Orange Line 4
ISBN 978-3-12-547544-1

GK **6 The story of the Allertons – passengers on the Mayflower**

Fill in the right verbs from the boxes in the simple past.

decide   leave   give   live (2x)   go   marry   have   hear   want   meet

Mary Norris first __lived__ in Newbury, England. In 1609 she _____ to Holland.

Mary's family _____ England when the religious oppression there became stronger.

In Leiden, Holland, the young woman _____ Isaac Allerton. They _____ in

1611 and Mary _____ birth to a boy (Bartholomew) in 1613 and to two girls (Remember

and Mary) in 1614 and 1616. The Allertons _____ another child early in 1620. But the

baby _____ **not** _____ long. It died in February 1620. Some weeks later they

_____ the news about the Mayflower's journey to America. First they _____ **not**

_____ to leave Holland. But later they _____ to emigrate on the Mayflower.

EK **6 The story of Mary and Mary – two passengers on the Mayflower**

a) *Fill in the verbs in the past perfect.*

Mary Norris (✱1590 – ✝1621) _____ *(to live)* in Newbury, England before

her family went to Holland in 1609. Mary's parents _____ *(to decide)* to leave

England when the religious oppression there became stronger. Mary met Isaac Allerton and after

they _____ *(to marry)* in 1611, Mary gave birth to a boy and two girls (1613,

1614 and 1616). The Allertons had another child in 1620 who died. The family decided to start a

new life in a different country after the family _____ *(to bury)* their baby on

5th February, 1620. They _____ *(to lose)* a child, but they

_____ *(to not lose)* hope of a better life somewhere else. After they

_____ *(to hear)* about the Mayflower's journey to America, their plan

to emigrate was clear.

b) *Complete the text with the right verb forms. Use the simple past or the past perfect.*

Before the Mayflower _____ in America on 11th November, 1620, Mary

Allerton (✱1616 – ✝1699) and her family _____ two months on the ship and

they _____ for some days *(arrive/spend/not eat)*. Life _____

easy for little Mary during those two months, but it even worse soon *(not be/become)*.

Orange Line 4
ISBN 978-3-12-547544-1

© Ernst Klett Verlag GmbH, Stuttgart 2008 | www.klett.de
Von dieser Druckvorlage ist die Vervielfältigung für den eigenen Unterrichtsgebrauch
gestattet. Die Kopiergebühren sind abgegolten. Alle Rechte vorbehalten.

Two days before Christmas Eve Mary's mother _____ birth to a boy who was

dead *(give)*. Two months later, on 25th February, 1621, Mary's mother _____

because the winter _____ too hard *(die/be)*.

By the end of March 1621 half of the 102 passengers on the Mayflower _____

but little Mary _____ to a very old age *(die/live)*. In 1636 Mary Allerton married

Thomas Cushman. They had seven children and at least 50 grandchildren.

EK **7 Thomas Cushman**

Write five sentences in the past perfect about Thomas Cushman's trip to America. Look at the clues.

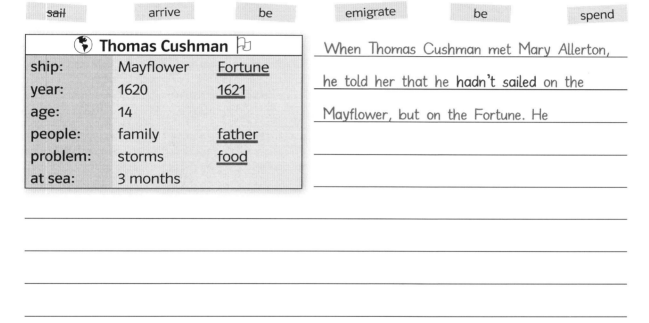

sail   arrive   be   emigrate   be   spend

🌐 Thomas Cushman 🗺		
ship:	Mayflower	Fortune
year:	1620	1621
age:	14	
people:	family	father
problem:	storms	food
at sea:	3 months	

When Thomas Cushman met Mary Allerton,
he told her that he hadn't sailed on the
Mayflower, but on the Fortune. He

EK **8 . . . before they emigrated?**

Ask five questions to find out about Thomas's life before he and his father emigrated to America.
Use the past perfect.

1. where • they • live   2. how • Thomas's life • be   3. what school • he • go to

4. how • he • feel about his father's plan   5. why • his mother • not come with them

1. Where had they lived before they emigrated?

2. _____

3. _____

4. _____

5. _____

 © Ernst Klett Verlag GmbH, Stuttgart 2008 | www.klett.de
Von dieser Druckvorlage ist die Vervielfältigung für den eigenen Unterrichtsgebrauch
gestattet. Die Kopiergebühren sind abgegolten. Alle Rechte vorbehalten.

Orange Line 4
ISBN 978-3-12-547544-1

9 What a day!

GK *Send an e-mail to Kate. Tell her about your busy day yesterday. Write at least four sentences. Look at the clues.*

I • come home from school at ... and • drink tea
then • Mum • tell me to go shopping
after that • ... • ask me to help ... with the ...
when I • want to wash my hair • ... • come to see me

Hi Kate,

Yesterday was a really busy day! I came home

from school at 4 o'clock and

EK *Send an e-mail to Kate. Tell her about your busy day yesterday. Write at least three sentences.*
Write   • what you had just done, when ...
*   • what happened after you had done it.*
Look at the clues.

I • just • come home from school when	Mum • tell me to go shopping
after • I • come back	? • ask me to help ... with the ...
I • just • wash my hair when ...	? • come to see me
after • ? • leave	telephone • ring
...	...

Hi Kate,

Yesterday was a really busy day! I had just

come home from school when Mum told me

to go shopping. After I had come back,

Orange Line 4
ISBN 978-3-12-547544-1
© Ernst Klett Verlag GmbH, Stuttgart 2008 | www.klett.de
Von dieser Druckvorlage ist die Vervielfältigung für den eigenen Unterrichtsgebrauch gestattet. Die Kopiergebühren sind abgegolten. Alle Rechte vorbehalten.

Klett

10 NYC crossword puzzle

GK

Across ⇨
1. The Statue of Liberty is a symbol of …
4. The Statue of Liberty is in NY … (AE)
6. The Empire State Building is the tallest … in NYC.
8. NYC has five of them. (plural)
9. There are a lot of them on Times Square. (AE/plural)
10. During Spring Festival people in Chinatown have a big … with huge dragons in the streets.

Down ⇩
2. During Spring Festival people in Chinatown put red paper … in the windows and doors. (plural)
3. Chinatown in Manhattan is a famous … (AE)
5. During Spring Festival people in Chinatown have … to frighten monsters away. (plural)
7. These people run everywhere in NYC. (plural)

EK

Down ⇩
1. The Empire State Building is the tallest … in NYC.
2. The Statue of Liberty is a symbol of …
3. During Spring Festival people in Chinatown have … to frighten monsters away. (plural)
4. These people run everywhere in NYC. (plural)
7. During Spring Festival people in Chinatown put red paper … in the windows and doors. (plural)
8. There are a lot of them on Times Square. (AE/plural)

Across ⇨
5. NYC has five of them. (plural)
6. Chinatown in Manhattan is a famous … (AE)
9. The Mohawks, who often helped to build the NY skyscrapers, are … (two words/plural)
10. During Spring Festival people in Chinatown have a big …with huge dragons.
11. The Statue of Liberty is in NY … (AE)

© Ernst Klett Verlag GmbH, Stuttgart 2008 | www.klett.de
Von dieser Druckvorlage ist die Vervielfältigung für den eigenen Unterrichtsgebrauch gestattet. Die Kopiergebühren sind abgegolten. Alle Rechte vorbehalten.

Orange Line 4
ISBN 978-3-12-547544-1

11 Immigration words

Complete the sentences with the right "immigration" words.

GK After 1620 more and more people from Europe left their home countries.

They _e_____d_ because they hoped to have a better life in the New World.

Many of them wanted to escape from _f_____ because they did not have enough to eat.

Others wanted to escape from _w_____ or _o_____ because there was no peace

or freedom in their countries.

From 1892 to 1954 about 12 million _i_____ landed at Ellis Island.

In 1921 the US started _q_____ for people who wanted to enter the country.

EK After 1620 more and more people from Europe left their home countries. They _e_____d_

because they hoped to have a better life in the New World.

Many of them wanted to escape from _f_____ and _p_____ because they did

not have enough to eat and were very poor.

Others wanted to escape from _w_____ or _o_____ because there was no peace

or freedom in their countries.

Their journey across the Atlantic Ocean was often terrible. A lot of the passengers were

_s_____ when the weather was stormy.

From 1892 to 1954 about 12 million _i_____ landed at Ellis Island.

In 1921 the US started _q_____ for people who wanted to enter the country.

In 1954 they closed the _i_____ station on Ellis Island.

EK ## 12 British English (BE) – American English (AE)

What is it in American English? Put the pairs into the right boxes. Look at the examples.

centre – …   chips – …   colour – …   favourite – …   harbour – …

holiday – …   neighbourhood – …   theatre – …   policeman – …   flat – …

BE	AE
centre	center

BE	AE
colour	color

BE	AE
flat	apartment

Orange Line 4
ISBN 978-3-12-547544-1

© Ernst Klett Verlag GmbH, Stuttgart 2008 | www.klett.de
Von dieser Druckvorlage ist die Vervielfältigung für den eigenen Unterrichtsgebrauch
gestattet. Die Kopiergebühren sind abgegolten. Alle Rechte vorbehalten.

Klett

GK + EK **13 US money**

What do you call them?

5 cents	10 cents	25 cents	100 cents
_____	_____	_____	_____

GK + EK **14 A flight in a helicopter**

Complete the sentences with the right word. Look at the boxes.

zyzdi	nyerecmeg	~~pilto~~	raxel	riapers	raro	eastk fof

1. The person who flies a helicopter is the _pilot_____ .

2. When you start a helicopter, you can hear the engines _____ .

3. When a helicopter goes up into the air, it _____ _____ .

4. Before a helicopter can start, a technical team checks everything and _____

    anything that is not OK.

5. A helicopter flight is nothing for people who feel _____ or sick when they are

    high up in the air.

6. In an _____ you must listen to what the pilot says and stay calm.

EK 7. Passengers on a helicopter should try to _____ so that they can enjoy the

    spectacular views.

K + EK **15 Food words**

Put the food words into the right boxes. Look at the examples.

bacon	cream cheese	~~biscuits~~	cherry	bagel	Danish	cupcake
French fries	maple syrup	pancake	pastrami	~~sausage~~	~~strawberry~~	turkey

sweet food	food that comes from animals	food that comes from plants or trees
biscuits	sausage	strawberry

 © Ernst Klett Verlag GmbH, Stuttgart 2008 | www.klett.de
Von dieser Druckvorlage ist die Vervielfältigung für den eigenen Unterrichtsgebrauch
gestattet. Die Kopiergebühren sind abgegolten. Alle Rechte vorbehalten.

Orange Line 4
ISBN 978-3-12-547544-1

GK + EK **16 Everyday English: At a deli with a friend**

Complete the dialogue. Order drinks and food for two people.

FOOD

Turkey bagel	$5.00
Cheese sandwich	$3.95
Fruit salad	$4.50
Cupcake	$2.00

DRINKS

Cappuccino	$3.00
Tea	$2.00
Big Coke	$3.50
Water	$1.80

You: Hi, we'd like _____   *Order something to eat for two.*

_____

Waiter: Here you are. Would you like to have anything to drink?

You: Yes, please. _____   *Order something to drink for two.*

_____

Waiter: Anything else?

You: _____   *Order something else.*

_____

Waiter: OK. That's _____ dollars _____ cents, please!

You: _____   *Talk about the change.*

_____

GK **17 Live and work in NYC?**

Write a text. Would you like to live and work in New York City. Why/Why not?

☺	☹
• fantastic	• busy
• interesting people	• crowds everywhere
• good jobs	• long way to work
• the best shops	• poor/expensive
• lots of fun	• lonely
• ...	• ...

_____

_____

_____

_____

_____

_____

_____

Orange Line 4
ISBN 978-3-12-547544-1

© Ernst Klett Verlag GmbH, Stuttgart 2008 | www.klett.de
Von dieser Druckvorlage ist die Vervielfältigung für den eigenen Unterrichtsgebrauch gestattet. Die Kopiergebühren sind abgegolten. Alle Rechte vorbehalten.

EK **17 Mixed bag: How it all started**

Complete the text with the best words.

You know that …

- NYC has a _____ of 8.8 million and is the place with the highest number of people in the US.

- it is also the largest US city with five big _____ like the Bronx, Brooklyn or Manhattan and hundreds of _____ e.g. Chinatown, Greenwich Village or Harlem.

But did you also know that …

- the Lenapi people (the Delaware Indians) _____ on Manhattan Island and in the area around long _____ European people arrived?

- the Lenapi were a group of different _____ _____ spoke a similar language?

- in 1614 some rich people from Holland came and _____ a town which they called 'New Amsterdam' later? One of _____, Peter Minuit, made history.

- in 1626 this _____ man bought Manhattan Island from the Lenapi _____ $24?

- in 1664 the English won over the Dutch in the first English-Dutch _____ from 1652 to 1654, and called the place 'New York'?

- by 1700 hundreds of English and Dutch people _____ to New York, but there were only 200 Lenapi people left _____ the area?

 © Ernst Klett Verlag GmbH, Stuttgart 2008 | www.klett.de
Von dieser Druckvorlage ist die Vervielfältigung für den eigenen Unterrichtsgebrauch gestattet. Die Kopiergebühren sind abgegolten. Alle Rechte vorbehalten.

Orange Line 4
ISBN 978-3-12-547544-1

GK **18 Mediation and communication: Dreaming the American dream?**

You and a friend find this information on the Internet.

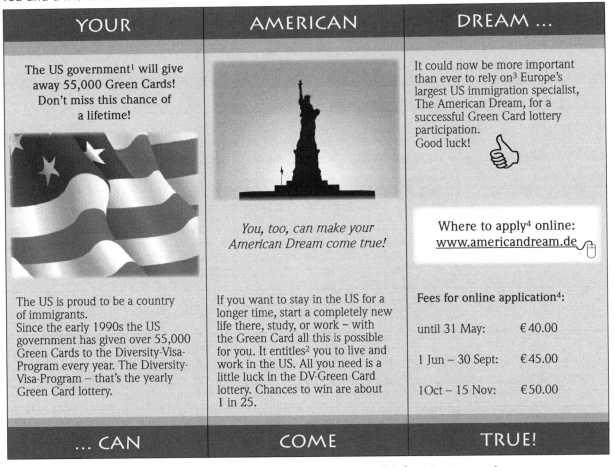

YOUR · AMERICAN · DREAM ...

The US government[1] will give away 55,000 Green Cards! Don't miss this chance of a lifetime!

The US is proud to be a country of immigrants.
Since the early 1990s the US government has given over 55,000 Green Cards to the Diversity-Visa-Program every year. The Diversity-Visa-Program – that's the yearly Green Card lottery.

You, too, can make your American Dream come true!

If you want to stay in the US for a longer time, start a completely new life there, study, or work – with the Green Card all this is possible for you. It entitles[2] you to live and work in the US. All you need is a little luck in the DV-Green Card lottery. Chances to win are about 1 in 25.

It could now be more important than ever to rely on[3] Europe's largest US immigration specialist, The American Dream, for a successful Green Card lottery participation.
Good luck!

Where to apply[4] online:
www.americandream.de

Fees for online application[4]:

until 31 May:	€ 40.00
1 Jun – 30 Sept:	€ 45.00
1 Oct – 15 Nov:	€ 50.00

... CAN · COME · TRUE!

[1]government ['gʌvənmənt] – *Regierung*; [2]to entitle [ɪn'taɪtl] – *berechtigen*; [3]to rely on [rɪ'laɪ] – *sich verlassen auf,*
[4]to apply/application [ə'plaɪ/ˌæplɪ'keɪʃən] – *sich bewerben/Bewerbung*

Your friend doesn't speak English. Answer his/her questions.

1. Wozu braucht man eine Green Card in den USA?

_____

2. Wie kann man sie erwerben?

_____

3. Wie viele Green Cards stehen zur Verfügung und welche Chancen hat man?

_____

4. Wo bewirbt man sich?

_____

5. Kostet das etwas?

_____

Orange Line 4
ISBN 978-3-12-547544-1

© Ernst Klett Verlag GmbH, Stuttgart 2008 | www.klett.de
Von dieser Druckvorlage ist die Vervielfältigung für den eigenen Unterrichtsgebrauch
gestattet. Die Kopiergebühren sind abgegolten. Alle Rechte vorbehalten.

Klett

EK 18 Mediation and communication: A trip to New York

Situation: Deine Großeltern planen eine Kurzreise nach New York. Hilf ihnen zu entscheiden, ob sie das Ground Zero Museum Workshop besuchen.

Ground Zero Museum Workshop • Experience the 'REAL' Ground Zero

Ground Zero Museum Workshop, the "biggest little museum in New York", is open every day. Your visit to New York will not be complete without a trip to this special little museum. Most visitors who want to learn more about 11th September and the time after come to this museum BEFORE going to the former World Trade Center site.

The museum was inspired by Mr Suson who decided to build a museum that would help visitors to NYC understand what went on "inside" Ground Zero.

Permanent Exhibit of pictures, artifacts & video from the Ground Zero Recovery

Address:
420 West 14th street, Floor 2
(between 9th Avenue &
Washington Street)
Tel. (212) 924-1040

We are located 8 minutes from Ground Zero by cab or subway.

For a downloadable NYC MAP click here.
E-mail:
GroundZeroMuseum@aol.com

Tour times:
Sunday and Monday:
12:00 Noon, 2:00 p.m., 4:00 p.m.
Tuesday:
11:00 a.m., 1:00 p.m., 3:00 p.m.
Wednesday:
–
Thursday to Saturday:
11:00 a.m., 1:00 p.m., 3:00 p.m.
Give us a call and we will arrange a tour for you!

PLEASE ARRIVE ONLY 5 MINUTES BEFORE TOUR TIME
CAMERAS: ☑ YES   VIDEOTAPING: ☒ NO

Admission:
* $19.00 per person for the 90 min. tour
* $16.00 for Senior Citizens (65+) and children 12 and under
* Special group rates for 20 or more

1. Was bezweckt das Museum und was kann man dort sehen?

_____

2. Wo befindet sich das Museum?

_____

3. Gibt es deutschsprachige Führungen?

_____

4. Ist es täglich geöffnet?

_____

5. Was kostet der Eintritt?

_____

6. Kann man dort Fotos machen oder filmen?

_____

 Klett © Ernst Klett Verlag GmbH, Stuttgart 2008 | www.klett.de
Von dieser Druckvorlage ist die Vervielfältigung für den eigenen Unterrichtsgebrauch gestattet. Die Kopiergebühren sind abgegolten. Alle Rechte vorbehalten.

Orange Line 4
ISBN 978-3-12-547544-1

Unit 2   A new school year

🔊 1 Let's listen: The art of dating

GK a) *Complete the sentences with the right word(s).*

1. Ryan is practising how to ask _____ for a date.

2. Ryan is doing it in the _____ .

EK a) *Complete the sentences with the right word(s).*

1. Ryan is _____ how to ask Anna for a date.

2. Ryan is doing it in the bathroom, in front of the _____ .

3. Ryan is doing it because he _____ Anna yet.

GK + EK b) *What is Ryan worrying about? Tick the <u>four</u> right boxes (✔).*

Ryan is worrying …

1. that Anna will say 'no' to a date with him.	
2. that Anna will laugh at him.	
3. that somebody else has already asked Anna for a date.	
4. that he should send Anna a letter.	
5. because he can't dance.	
6. that Anna hates football.	
EK 7. that Tony will ask her for a date.	

GK + EK c) *What is so funny about the ending? Tick (✔) the right box.*

1. Tony asks the girl for a date.
2. Ryan is really nervous when he sees the girl at the door.
3. The girl asks Ryan for a date before Ryan can do it.

GK + EK d) *What do you think of Tony's answers?*

_____

2 Let's read: Make a Difference Day

GK + EK "What shall we do on 'Make a Difference Day'?" asked James.
"Oh, I don't know. I never have any good ideas," said Sandra.

EK "Well, I think we should do something that makes school better,"
said James. "Yes, that would be nice but I'd like to collect some
money for the children's home or the old people's home, too," said
Bob. "Maybe we could do both," answered James. "We could do
something at school that people pay for and then we could give
the money to the old people's home." "Like what?" said Sandra.
"Well, we could get some orange trees and put them in the school
garden. They look nice and we could sell the oranges," said James. "But where do we get orange trees   10
from? Aren't they expensive?" asked Bob. "Hm, I don't know. You haven't said anything, Nicole. What
do you want to do?"

Make a Difference Day   5

Orange Line 4
ISBN 978-3-12-547544-1
© Ernst Klett Verlag GmbH, Stuttgart 2008 | www.klett.de
Von dieser Druckvorlage ist die Vervielfältigung für den eigenen Unterrichtsgebrauch
gestattet. Die Kopiergebühren sind abgegolten. Alle Rechte vorbehalten.

GK + EK "Nothing. I haven't got time," answered Nicole. "I've got to work every Saturday."
"But you can't do nothing," said James. "Everyone does something on 'Make a Difference Day'."
"Not me," answered Nicole. "I've got too much to do, and why should I give money or my time to 15 other people? I need the money, too. My dad has lost his job. We've never had a holiday. And I have to work every week if I want something."
"Yes, but there are people out there who can't work. They haven't got any money or enough food to eat," said James.
"Well, let the rich people give them some money," shouted Nicole who was angry now. She walked 20 home and felt angry all the way. Why should she give her time and money? She needed the money. She worked every week and didn't have enough time for her homework, and she wanted a new bike. She thought about life and how unfair it was. She thought about all the things that she wanted and couldn't have.

The next day at school her friends talked again about "Make a Difference Day" again but Nicole didn't 25 say anything. Then James said, "I know. Let's go to the children's home and see what they want and what they need. Then maybe we'll have an idea." They all thought it was a good idea and they all went after school on Friday. Nicole went, too, because she wanted to go for a pizza with them later. She didn't really want to see the children's home and when she got there, she wanted to leave again right away because she felt so sad. For the first time she understood how much she had. 30

EK a) *Read the text and find out which of the pupils it is. Tick (✔) the right box(es).*

Who …	James	Sandra	Bob	Nicole
1. has no idea what they can do?				
2. thinks it is important to do something for their school?				
3. thinks it is important to help a special group of people?				
4. thinks that they could do something for their school and for a special group of people at the same time?				
5. wants to know how they can do both?				
6. makes an interesting suggestion?				
7. sees the problems with that suggestion?				
8. does not take part in "Make a Difference Day"?				
9. thinks that everyone should take part in "Make a Difference Day"?				
10. suggests that they may get an idea for "Make a Difference Day" when they visit the children's home?				
11. visits the children's home?				
12. goes to the children's home for her own reason[1]?				

[1]reason ['riːzn] – *Grund*

GK + EK b) *Find the right ending to the six sentences. Draw lines.*

1. Nicole does not want to …	A) she should give her time to others.
2. One reason for this is that …	B) there are people who have bigger problems than Nicole has.
3. So Nicole does not see why …	C) her family has money problems.
4. Also she needs the extra money because …	D) do anything on "Make A Difference Day".
5. James thinks that …	E) the rich people should help with money.
6. But Nicole is angry and says that …	F) she usually works on Saturdays.

© Ernst Klett Verlag GmbH, Stuttgart 2008 | www.klett.de
Von dieser Druckvorlage ist die Vervielfältigung für den eigenen Unterrichtsgebrauch gestattet. Die Kopiergebühren sind abgegolten. Alle Rechte vorbehalten.

Orange Line 4
ISBN 978-3-12-547544-1

GK + EK c) *Tick (✔) the right box.*

On her way home, Nicole was angry because …
1. James did not understand how important the extra money was for her.
2. she could not have all the things that she wanted although she worked so hard.
3. she thought that other people were luckier than she was.

GK d) *Answer the questions.*

1. Where did the friends go on Friday?

    _____

2. Why did Nicole go with them?

    _____

3. How did Nicole feel there and what did she learn?

    _____

EK d) *Answer the questions.*

1. Why does Nicole think life is unfair?

    _____

2. What event helps Nicole to see her situation differently?

    _____

EK ### 3 Mixed bag: Pizza after their visit to the children's home?

Fill in the best words.

Sandra: Let's go to Tonio's. They've the best pizzas in town.

Bob: I don't want a pizza after all the things we've _____ at the children's home.

Sandra: You're _____. It was your idea to have a pizza after we had been to the children's

home, _____ it?

Nicole: I think Bob is right. We _____ spend our money at a pizza shop, but save it

_____ our "Make a Difference Day" project.

James: What _____ going to my place? We could think _____ our project.

Nicole: Don't you think we should first ask the children's home for _____ to do

a project there? They _____ not want it.

James: Yes, you're right. We'd better _____ the director before we begin. Does anyone

_____ his e-mail address or phone number?

Sandra: Why not try and see him now? If we're _____, he'll still be in his office.

Bob: I think we should make a _____ with him. He may _____ very busy.

Orange Line 4
ISBN 978-3-12-547544-1
© Ernst Klett Verlag GmbH, Stuttgart 2008 | www.klett.de
Von dieser Druckvorlage ist die Vervielfältigung für den eigenen Unterrichtsgebrauch
gestattet. Die Kopiergebühren sind abgegolten. Alle Rechte vorbehalten.

GK + EK **4 Ready for the date?**

Write what Brenda has done, what Leroy has done and what they both have done.
Look at the example.

Brenda		Leroy
	buy some chocolate	✓
✓	choose a teddy bear	
	put some money in (his/her/their) wallet	✓
✓	pack (his/her/their) bag	
✓	do (his/her/their) hair	✓
✓	clean (his/her/their) shoes	
✓	tell (his/her/their) parents about the date	✓
	ask (his/her/their) mum to pick them up at 10 p.m.	✓

EK

Leroy has bought some chocolate for Brenda. Brenda _____

_____

_____

_____

_____

GK + EK **5 Oh, Mum!**

a) *Leroy's mum wants Leroy to have a nice date. Write his mum's questions. Use the present perfect.*

1.	you/buy/anything nice for Brenda	✓
2.	what/you/buy/for her	–
3.	you/put on/a nice T-shirt	✓
4.	you and Dad/clean/the car	✗
5.	your sister/print/the photo for Brenda	✗
6.	your grandparents/give/you/any extra money	✗
7.	whose aftershave/you/put on – Mike's or Dad's	–
8.	you/tell/Brenda's parents that I'll pick you up	✗

1. Have you _____

_____

_____

_____

_____

_____

_____

EK

_____

_____

_____

_____

 © Ernst Klett Verlag GmbH, Stuttgart 2008 | www.klett.de
Von dieser Druckvorlage ist die Vervielfältigung für den eigenen Unterrichtsgebrauch gestattet. Die Kopiergebühren sind abgegolten. Alle Rechte vorbehalten.

Orange Line 4
ISBN 978-3-12-547544-1   23

b) *Write what Leroy and the rest of the family haven't done yet. Use the present perfect and 'yet'.*

Leroy and his dad haven't cleaned the car yet.

6 Over to you!

a) *Write five interesting questions you could ask your date. Use the present perfect and 'ever'.*
Look at the verbs in the boxes for some ideas.

GK   be • been   dare to (reg.)   hear • heard   feel • felt   try • tried to   visit (reg.)

EK   be   dare to   hear   feel   try to   visit   ...

Have Has	you		
	your family	ever	... ?
	your brother/ sister/class ...		
	...		

GK b) *Now tell your date what you have already done and have never done before.*
Use the present perfect and 'already' and 'never'. Write four sentences.

EK b) *Now tell your date what you/your best friend have/has already done and have/has never done*
before, but would like to do. Use the present perfect and 'already' and 'never'. Write six sentences.

Orange Line 4
ISBN 978-3-12-547544-1
© Ernst Klett Verlag GmbH, Stuttgart 2008 | www.klett.de
Von dieser Druckvorlage ist die Vervielfältigung für den eigenen Unterrichtsgebrauch
gestattet. Die Kopiergebühren sind abgegolten. Alle Rechte vorbehalten.

Klett

GK **7 School rules**

Write about the rules at your school. Use 'must', 'mustn't', 'needn't', 'can' and 'can't'.
Look at the clues or use your own ideas. Write at least six rules.

1. + 2.	wear			...
3. + 4.			... in the lessons	
5. + 6.			... at school	
7. + 8.	bring		... to school	

1. You must wear school

2. You mustn't wear

EK **7 What could you say?**

Your friend is in a difficult situation. Try to help and give some advice. Write three sentences for each
situation. Use 'should', 'shouldn't', 'may', 'may not', 'must' and 'mustn't'.

1. Your friend's date was no success. She's very unhappy. She's crying and calling herself a jerk.	1. You shouldn't
2. Your friend has got an invitation to a formal party. He doesn't know what to wear and how to do ballroom dancing.	2.
3. Your friend wants to get on the cheerleader's team. There are some other attractive girls who are fit and have good chances.	3.

 © Ernst Klett Verlag GmbH, Stuttgart 2008 | www.klett.de
Von dieser Druckvorlage ist die Vervielfältigung für den eigenen Unterrichtsgebrauch
gestattet. Die Kopiergebühren sind abgegolten. Alle Rechte vorbehalten.

Orange Line 4
ISBN 978-3-12-547544-1

EK **8 The art of dating**

Complete the text with survival tips. Use 'should', 'shouldn't', 'may', 'may not', 'must' and 'mustn't'.

♥ **THE ART OF DATING** ♥

You like someone and want to go out with him or her? Well, you better learn quick!

☺ direct ☹ take too long ✗ be bored	*» How to ask:* You should always ask him or her in a direct way. You shouldn't take too long. Your partner may be bored.
☺ wash ☹ strange clothes ✗ think that you belong to a gang	*» What to do before:*
☺ arrive on time/ do what you both like ☹ be late/say too much ✗ believe that not interested/ honest and thoughtful	*» When you go on the date:*
☺ say something nice ☹ lie about your feelings ✗ be embarrassed	*» How to end the date:*

9 Everyday English

What do you say in these situations?

GK 1. You meet a friend. _____

2. You want so say something nice to a partner. _____

3. Your partner thinks of you and your wishes. _____

4. You leave someone who you will see again later. _____

EK 1. You leave someone who you will see again later. _____

2. You meet a friend. _____

3. You don't believe what someone has just said. _____

4. Your friend is very sad. _____

5. Something tastes or feels horrible. _____

Orange Line 4
ISBN 978-3-12-547544-1

© Ernst Klett Verlag GmbH, Stuttgart 2008 | www.klett.de
Von dieser Druckvorlage ist die Vervielfältigung für den eigenen Unterrichtsgebrauch
gestattet. Die Kopiergebühren sind abgegolten. Alle Rechte vorbehalten.

GK + EK **10 Everyday English: Dating someone**

Complete the dialogue.

You: _____   *Say hello and ask*
_____   *your partner for*
   a date.

Partner: Oh yes, that would be great.

You: _____   *Tell your partner*
_____   *when you'll pick*
   him/her up from
_____   *home.*

EK Partner: Well, can't we meet somewhere else?

You: _____   *Suggest a place*
_____   *where you can*
   meet.

Partner: OK. That would be fine.

You: _____   *Tell him/her*
   something nice.

Partner: Thanks.

You: _____   *Say goodbye in*
   a warm way.

11 What a day!

GK *Imagine you had a date today. Write four sentences or more about it in your diary.*

EK *Imagine you had a date today. Write six sentences or more about it in your diary.*

Write about

- *the awful film that you saw,*

- *the snack bar that you went to,*

- *the friends who you met,*

- *the nice evening that you had.*

_____ (date)

Dear Diary, _____

_____

_____

_____

_____

_____

_____

_____

_____

_____

© Ernst Klett Verlag GmbH, Stuttgart 2008 | www.klett.de
Von dieser Druckvorlage ist die Vervielfältigung für den eigenen Unterrichtsgebrauch
gestattet. Die Kopiergebühren sind abgegolten. Alle Rechte vorbehalten.

Orange Line 4
ISBN 978-3-12-547544-1

GK + EK **12 School in GB and the US**

Look at the British school words and write down what they are in the US.

in GB	in the US
(5–11) primary school	(5–11)
(11–16) comprehensive or grammar school (lower school)	(11–14)
(16–18) comprehensive or grammar school (upper school)	(14–18)
pupil	
year	
mark	
EK break	

GK + EK **13 Traditions at US schools**

Write down the right words.

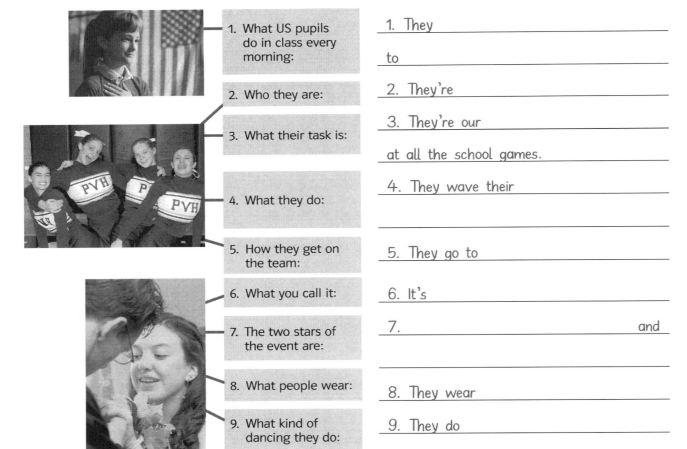

1. What US pupils do in class every morning:

2. Who they are:

3. What their task is:

4. What they do:

5. How they get on the team:

6. What you call it:

7. The two stars of the event are:

8. What people wear:

9. What kind of dancing they do:

1. They _____

   to _____

2. They're _____

3. They're our _____

   at all the school games.

4. They wave their _____

   _____

5. They go to _____

6. It's _____

7. _____ and

   _____

8. They wear _____

9. They do _____

Orange Line 4
ISBN 978-3-12-547544-1

© Ernst Klett Verlag GmbH, Stuttgart 2008 | www.klett.de
Von dieser Druckvorlage ist die Vervielfältigung für den eigenen Unterrichtsgebrauch
gestattet. Die Kopiergebühren sind abgegolten. Alle Rechte vorbehalten.

14 Adjectives with a positive, negative or neutral meaning

GK + EK a) *Sort the adjectives into the best group. Look at the example.*

awful   attractive   awesome   clumsy   brand new

formal   honest   public   mean   thoughtful

EK   absent   hurtful   kind   straight   embarrassing

positive meaning ☺	negative meaning ☹	neutral meaning ☺
		formal

GK + EK b) *Choose six of the adjectives and use them to make good phrases. Look at the example.*

formal dress,

15 Nouns

GK *Write down the right noun from the boxes. Be careful. There are four nouns too many!*

absence   curriculum   jerk   rally   supporter

advert   difference   permission   rival   tryout

EK *Fill in the right nouns.*

1. When something is not the same like something else, there is a _____

   between them.

2. If students have been ill, they have to bring an _____ slip to school.

3. Someone who cheers for you and helps you is a _____.

4. When someone says that you can do something, you have _____ to do it.

5. It is not nice to call someone a _____ because he is clumsy.

6. Someone who fights for or wants to have something that you want is your _____.

EK 7. You call a short text under a picture or cartoon a _____.

EK 8. Someone who is older than 18 is an _____.

 © Ernst Klett Verlag GmbH, Stuttgart 2008 | www.klett.de
Von dieser Druckvorlage ist die Vervielfältigung für den eigenen Unterrichtsgebrauch
gestattet. Die Kopiergebühren sind abgegolten. Alle Rechte vorbehalten.

Orange Line 4
ISBN 978-3-12-547544-1

16 Verbs

Match each verb with a phrase.

GK

| something dangerous | a photo | an exam | school | going red in the face |

| a date | blue jeans | the homecoming queen |

to dare to do	_____	to lie without	_____
to end	_____	to wear	_____
to graduate from	_____	to pass	_____
to have a look at	_____	to vote for	_____

EK

| a dangerous thing | a photo | without getting red in the face | before a match |

| from school | a group | a story | time | an exam | the homecoming queen |

to belong to	_____	to pass	_____
to dare to do	_____	to think up	_____
to have a look at	_____	to vote for	_____
to graduate	_____	to warm up	_____
to lie	_____	to waste	_____

GK + EK ## 17 Mediation and communication

🖐🖐 MAKE A DIFFERENCE DAY 🖐🖐

⇨ Please mail by Nov. 16 or enter online at makeadifferenceday.com

AWARD ENTRY FORM

Your name: _____

Your organization: _____

Address: _____

City/State: _____

Phone: _____

E-mail address: _____

Send one picture that best illustrates your Make A Difference Day project and win a free vacation.

How many people:

took part? _____

did you help? _____

Check here if:

! you've taken part in MADD before

! you worked with a local center on this project

! your project was in the media (TV, radio, newspaper)

Orange Line 4
ISBN 978-3-12-547544-1
© Ernst Klett Verlag GmbH, Stuttgart 2008 | www.klett.de
Von dieser Druckvorlage ist die Vervielfältigung für den eigenen Unterrichtsgebrauch gestattet. Die Kopiergebühren sind abgegolten. Alle Rechte vorbehalten.

 Klett

👋👋 MAKE A DIFFERENCE DAY 👋👋

Mail this form by Nov. 16 to:
USA WEEKEND
MADD
7950 Weekend Drive
McLean, Va. 22107

On Make A Difference Day, this is what we did: _____

_____

_____

We decided to do this because: _____

_____

_____

What we did will really help people because: _____

_____

_____

Here's how we first heard about Make A Difference Day: _____

_____

_____

GK *Situation: Ein neuer Schüler in deiner Klasse spricht kaum Englisch.*
Hilf ihm das Formular zu verstehen. Beantworte seine Fragen.

EK *There's a new pupil in your class who doesn't speak much English because French was his first foreign*
language at the school he went to before. Help him. Read the text and answer his questions.

1. Was ist das für ein Formular?

   _____

2. Welche Angaben muss man machen?

   _____

   _____

   _____

3. Im Kleingedruckten rechts werden noch ein paar prinzipielle Dinge und Fakten abgefragt und die
   Anschrift gegeben. Stimmt's?

   _____

4. Können die Teilnehmer auch etwas gewinnen? Wenn ja, was und wie?

   _____

   _____

© Ernst Klett Verlag GmbH, Stuttgart 2008 | www.klett.de
Von dieser Druckvorlage ist die Vervielfältigung für den eigenen Unterrichtsgebrauch
gestattet. Die Kopiergebühren sind abgegolten. Alle Rechte vorbehalten.

Orange Line 4
ISBN 978-3-12-547544-1

Unit 3 Our smart world

🔊 1 Let's listen: Problems in a hotel

GK + EK a) *What's the guests' room number?* _____

GK + EK b) *Which <u>four</u> things in the hotel room are missing or need repair? Tick (✔) the right boxes.*

1. the shower
2. the plug for the sink
3. the socket and/or the hairdryer
4. the TV
5. the remote control for the TV
6. the phone
7. the faucet

GK c) *How helpful do you think the woman at reception is? Tick (✔) the right box.*

1. She's very helpful and does everything to help the guests.
2. She's not very helpful and asks and says stupid things.
3. She's not helpful, but very friendly.

EK c) *Which four things tell you that the receptionist is not very helpful? Tick (✔) the right boxes.*

1. She thinks a dripping faucet is no problem at all.
2. She thinks that the guests are tired and only need to sleep.
3. She tells the guests that they should go to bed early.
4. She doesn't see why the guests worry about the remote control if they want to sleep.
5. She tells the guests that they're making a fuss over nothing.
6. She asks the guests if they've put the plug of the hairdryer in the socket.
7. She'll only send somebody up the next morning.

GK + EK d) *Tick (✔) the right box.*

The end is funny because …

1. … the woman at reception and the guests are angry.
2. … the woman at reception thinks the guests are idiots.
3. … the woman at reception is glad that they don't need to repair anything because the guests are leaving the next morning.

GK + EK e) *Find a different title. Tick (✔) the right box.*

1. Why some hotels like one-night guests best
2. Why you should never stay at a cheap hotel in the country
3. Why expensive city hotels are better

2 Let's read: The aliens are coming

EK **A** "So, will you come and visit me?" Michael asks. Sarah thinks about it. She met Michael at a Christmas party at a friend's house last year and he has visited her a few times in England but she hasn't visited him yet. She has so much to do and she's worried that she won't like it where Michael lives. Sarah lives in London. She's lived there for two years and she still finds it exciting. She goes out almost every evening. She meets her friends and plays in a band. There are so many things that she wants to do and so little time to do them in. Michael lives in a little village on the north-west coast of Scotland and Sarah thinks it must be very boring. When she asks him what he has done that day, he says he has gone for a walk or watched the sea. That's not for her, she thinks, but she wants to know him better and she knows it's not fair for him to visit her every time.

5

Orange Line 4
ISBN 978-3-12-547544-1
© Ernst Klett Verlag GmbH, Stuttgart 2008 | www.klett.de
Von dieser Druckvorlage ist die Vervielfältigung für den eigenen Unterrichtsgebrauch
gestattet. Die Kopiergebühren sind abgegolten. Alle Rechte vorbehalten.

That's not for her, she thinks, but she wants to know him better and she knows it's not fair for him to visit her every time. "OK, I'll come," she answers.
They are sitting on a beach now and looking at the sea.   10

GK **A** Sarah is visiting her friend Michael in Scotland. They are sitting on a beach in the north and looking at the sea.

GK + EK **B** "I love it here," says Sarah. "It's so beautiful. And it's so quiet. You can only hear the sound of the   15
waves on the beach. You're very lucky to live here." She's been here two days now and she has never felt so good in all her life.
"Yes, I know I'm lucky. I love it here, too, but it's even nicer when you're here."
Sarah laughs. This is her first visit to Scotland and she loves it. She loves the mountains and the sea, the music and the people. They watch the boats on the water and the sun go down behind the sea.   20

C It's getting darker and they look at all the stars in the sky. Sarah has never seen so many stars. Then she sees a strange light. It's red and green and it's moving and it's getting bigger. There are lots of lights all over the sky. "What's that?" asks Sarah and she's a little scared.
"They're lights from alien's spaceships. They're coming to visit us, I think," answers Michael.
"Oh, don't be silly," answers Sarah. "You don't believe in aliens, do you?" "Don't you?" answers   25
Michael. "Look at all those stars up there and think of all the stars that we can't see and all the planets. There must be life out there, don't you think?" "No, I don't. If there were aliens, I'm sure many people would see them. There would be photos of them," says Sarah.
"But why? Why should they visit us? Maybe they come near us, watch us for some time and then leave again. Just think: Any time they come, there's war on our planet. People are killing each other.   30
Why should they land? So they just stay up there and watch us and then go home again." Sarah looks at the lights again in the sky. They are so beautiful. She lies on the grass and looks up and smiles.

GK a) *Read the text and write down …*

– who Sarah visits: _____

– where he lives: _____

– why Sarah likes it there: _____

_____

– what Sarah likes about the place: _____

b) *Find the right endings to the six sentences. Draw lines.*

1. Michael thinks that the strange lights are …	A) silly.
2. But Sarah does not …	B) there must be life out there.
3. She tells Michael not to be …	C) people would have photos of them.
4. All those stars up in the sky make Michael believe that …	D) come near the Earth, watch our planet and then leave again.
5. But Sarah thinks if there were aliens, …	E) from aliens' spaceships.
6. Michael believes that the aliens only …	F) believe in aliens.

c) *What does Michael think? Why do the aliens not visit our planet? Answer in sentences.*

_____

_____

© Ernst Klett Verlag GmbH, Stuttgart 2008 | www.klett.de
Von dieser Druckvorlage ist die Vervielfältigung für den eigenen Unterrichtsgebrauch gestattet. Die Kopiergebühren sind abgegolten. Alle Rechte vorbehalten.

Orange Line 4
ISBN 978-3-12-547544-1

EK a) *Read the text and write down ...*

– who Sarah visits: _____

– where Sarah lives: _____

– how long she has lived there: _____

– how she likes it there: _____

– what she does there very often: _____

– what she thinks is special about this place: _____

_____

b) *What does Sarah think and feel about the place where Michael lives?*

Only tick (✔) one box.

Before she goes there:

Michael's place can be exciting, too, and it's time that she went there. ☐
Michael's place is probably OK and she should go there soon. ☐
Michael's place is boring, but it's not fair that she has not been there yet. ☐

Tick (✔) the three right boxes.

When she is there:

She feels that the place is very much alive. ☐
She enjoys the quiet of the place. ☐
She notices what she has missed in the past years. ☐
The place makes her feel good. ☐
She starts to love Scotland, its music and people. ☐
She likes the evenings under the Scottish sky best. ☐

c) *Complete the following sentences with words or phrases from the text (part C).*

Michael thinks that the strange lights are _____.

But Sarah doesn't _____ and tells Michael not to be

_____. All those stars up in the sky, all the stars that you cannot see and all the planets –

they all make Michael believe that _____.

But again Sarah doesn't agree with him. She thinks that _____,

people would know that they exist.

d) *Explain what Michael thinks about the aliens and why they don't visit our planet.*
   Answer in sentences.

_____

_____

_____

Orange Line 4
ISBN 978-3-12-547544-1

© Ernst Klett Verlag GmbH, Stuttgart 2008 | www.klett.de
Von dieser Druckvorlage ist die Vervielfältigung für den eigenen Unterrichtsgebrauch
gestattet. Die Kopiergebühren sind abgegolten. Alle Rechte vorbehalten.

GK 3 Comparing adjectives

Complete the grid with the missing forms.

adjective (positive form)	comparative	superlative
	cleaner	
		(the) busiest
big		
	more expensive	
healthy		
	nicer	
		(the) most beautiful
good		
		(the) worst
	hotter	
exciting		

GK 4 Abby – Ebby – Ibby

Compare Abby, Ebby and Ibby. Choose from the adjectives in the boxes.

bad   boring   clumsy   exciting   funny   good

nice   old   popular   silly   smart   sporty

a) *Write what is the same. Use the positive form of the adjectives and "as ... as".*
   Write three sentences.

_____

_____

_____

© Ernst Klett Verlag GmbH, Stuttgart 2008 | www.klett.de
Von dieser Druckvorlage ist die Vervielfältigung für den eigenen Unterrichtsgebrauch
gestattet. Die Kopiergebühren sind abgegolten. Alle Rechte vorbehalten.

Orange Line 4
ISBN 978-3-12-547544-1

b) *Write what is different. Use the positive form of the adjectives and "not as … as".*
   Write three sentences.

_____

_____

_____

c) *Write what is different. Use the comparative form of the adjectives and "… than".*
   Write three sentences.

_____

_____

_____

d) *Write who is **the** … (best/silliest/…). Use the superlative form of the adjectives.*
   Write three sentences.

I think _____

_____

_____

GK ## 5 Rich people

Complete the text with the best forms of the adjectives.
Be careful. You also need " … than" (3x) and "as … as" (1x).

Everyone wants to be _____ *(rich)*. Of course, life is usually _____

(easy) when you have the money to buy what you want. But does a lot of money also make

you _____ *(happy)*? Are the _____ *(rich)* people in the world also

the _____ *(happy)* ones? Who knows? They can drive the _____

(expensive) cars. They can live in the _____ *(fine)* houses. They can eat the

_____ *(good)* food and wear the _____ *(modern)* clothes.

But their life is often _____ *(dangerous)* the life of people like you and me.

They don't live _____ *(safely)* other people do. Of course, when they are sick,

they can have _____ *(good doctors)* people with less money.

But if they are very _____ *(sick)*, they die just like other people do.

A lot of money or only very little – the _____ *(important)* thing is

that you do something for yourself. You are _____ *(good)* everyone else.

Orange Line 4
ISBN 978-3-12-547544-1
© Ernst Klett Verlag GmbH, Stuttgart 2008 | www.klett.de
Von dieser Druckvorlage ist die Vervielfältigung für den eigenen Unterrichtsgebrauch
gestattet. Die Kopiergebühren sind abgegolten. Alle Rechte vorbehalten.

EK **3 Double guessing game**

Complete the sentences. Use the passive. Look at the clues and find the scrambled words.

1. SUTARNCI
2. QEPMUTNIE
3. FAOTYCR
4. LASGESS
5. MALSP
6. TESRESC
7. TOSCATRR
8. FOSU

9. | 1 | 2 | 3 | H | 4 | 5 | 6 | 7 | 8 | 9 |

1. They __are often closed__ *(often/ to close)* when it gets dark outside.

2. It _____ *(to need)* if you want to explore something.

3. It's a large building where things _____ *(to make)*.

4. They _____ *(to wear)* by people who can't see well.

5. They _____ *(to switch on)* in rooms when it's too dark to see.

6. They _____ *(often/to discover)* by private investigators.

7. They _____ *(to use)* to plough fields.

8. They _____ *(often/to describe)* as flat things with green and red lights.

9. It _____ *(to find)* everywhere in our high-tech world.

EK **4 That's silly!**

a) *Make up the kids' questions. Use the passive.*
b) *Then give the answers. Use the passive in the negative and in the positive form. Use the phrases and words in the boxes.*

questions
1. a plug – put into a faucet???
2. adaptors – need when the batteries are dead???
3. a fridge – use to keep frozen[1] food???
4. astronauts in space – monitor by air traffic controllers???
5. spaceships – launch from space stations???
6. a robot – operate by a pacemaker???

answers
socket
different socket system
fresh food
doctors
space centers
remote control

1. Is a plug put into a faucet? – No! A plug isn't put into a faucet. It's put into a socket.

2. Are _____

3. _____

4. _____

_____ [1]frozen ['frəʊzn] – *gefroren*

 © Ernst Klett Verlag GmbH, Stuttgart 2008 | www.klett.de
Von dieser Druckvorlage ist die Vervielfältigung für den eigenen Unterrichtsgebrauch gestattet. Die Kopiergebühren sind abgegolten. Alle Rechte vorbehalten.

Orange Line 4
ISBN 978-3-12-547544-1

5. _____

   _____

6. _____

   _____

EK 5 What's that?

Ask five questions to find out what this is. Use the passive. Look at the clues.

1. what/the thing/use for	4. how/it/switch on and off
2. what/it/call	5. how/it/operate
3. where/things like that/need	6. where/those things/sell

1. What is the thing used for? _____

2. _____

3. _____

4. _____

5. _____

6. _____

EK 6 How strawberries are prepared for deep-freezing[1]

Explain how strawberries are prepared for deep-freezing. Write four sentences.
Use the passive. Look at the clues.

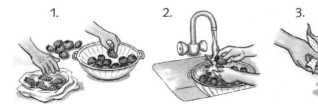

first	any bad strawberries/sort out	First any bad strawberries are sorted out. Then _____
then	wash/cold water/twice	_____
next	dry	_____
then	little green leaves/remove	_____
finally	put into/plastic[2] bags or boxes	_____

_____

[1]deep-freezing [ˌdiːpˈfriːzɪŋ] – *Tiefkühlen*, [2]plastic [ˈplæstɪk] – *Plastik*

Orange Line 4
ISBN 978-3-12-547544-1

© Ernst Klett Verlag GmbH, Stuttgart 2008 | www.klett.de
Von dieser Druckvorlage ist die Vervielfältigung für den eigenen Unterrichtsgebrauch
gestattet. Die Kopiergebühren sind abgegolten. Alle Rechte vorbehalten.

7 Space words

Do the puzzle.

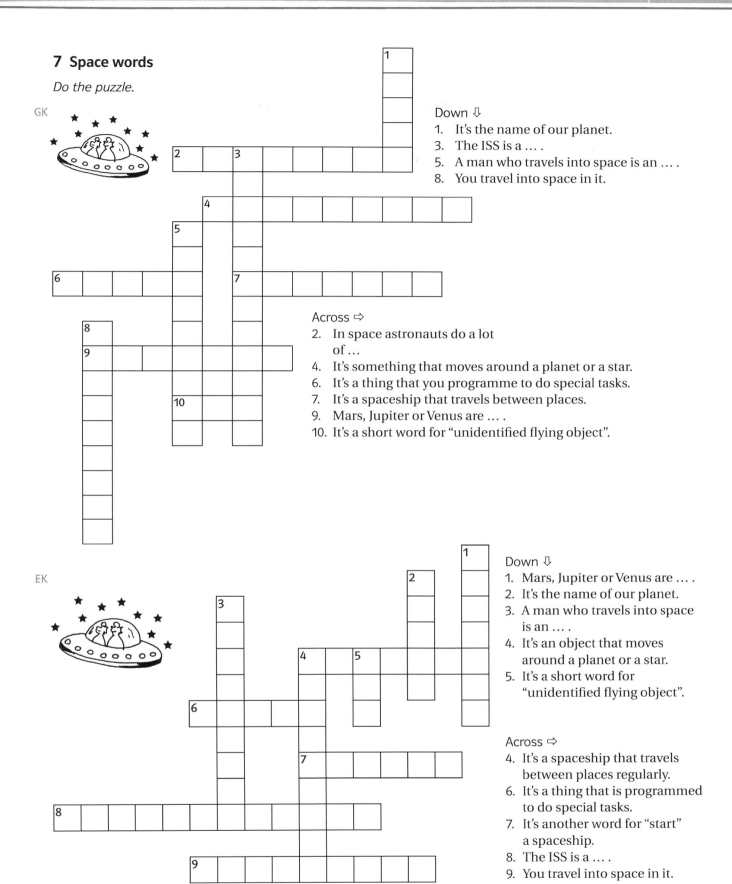

GK

Down ⇩
1. It's the name of our planet.
3. The ISS is a … .
5. A man who travels into space is an … .
8. You travel into space in it.

Across ⇨
2. In space astronauts do a lot of …
4. It's something that moves around a planet or a star.
6. It's a thing that you programme to do special tasks.
7. It's a spaceship that travels between places.
9. Mars, Jupiter or Venus are … .
10. It's a short word for "unidentified flying object".

EK

Down ⇩
1. Mars, Jupiter or Venus are … .
2. It's the name of our planet.
3. A man who travels into space is an … .
4. It's an object that moves around a planet or a star.
5. It's a short word for "unidentified flying object".

Across ⇨
4. It's a spaceship that travels between places regularly.
6. It's a thing that is programmed to do special tasks.
7. It's another word for "start" a spaceship.
8. The ISS is a … .
9. You travel into space in it.

© Ernst Klett Verlag GmbH, Stuttgart 2008 | www.klett.de
Von dieser Druckvorlage ist die Vervielfältigung für den eigenen Unterrichtsgebrauch gestattet. Die Kopiergebühren sind abgegolten. Alle Rechte vorbehalten.

Orange Line 4
ISBN 978-3-12-547544-1

8 Things in the house

Write down the words.

GK + EK

_____ _____ _____ _____ _____

_____ _____ _____ _____ _____

EK

_____ _____

9 Verbs

a) *Match the verbs with the best words or phrases.*

GK   a bomb   a field   food in the refrigerator   a meal   the lights   a machine   space   wet clothes

EK   a bomb   a dead battery   food in the refrigerator   one's hair   the lights   a machine   space   wet clothes

GK + EK   to explore _____   to keep _____

to defuse _____   to operate _____

GK   to dry _____   to plough _____

to cook _____   to turn on _____

EK   to cut off _____   to remove _____

to dry _____   to switch on _____

b) *Find the right word.*

GK   snaeil   an xaem   an cyagne   a buttabh   a tlobte

1. You can control it: _____

2. They may exist in space or on other

     planets: _____

3. It may drip: _____

4. You can fill it: _____

5. You can pass it: _____

EK   1. You can control it: _____

2. They may exist in space or on other

     planets: _____

3. It can leak: _____

4. It may flood when the washing machine

     breaks: _____

5. You can turn it on: _____

6. It may drip: _____

Orange Line 4
ISBN 978-3-12-547544-1

© Ernst Klett Verlag GmbH, Stuttgart 2008 | www.klett.de
Von dieser Druckvorlage ist die Vervielfältigung für den eigenen Unterrichtsgebrauch
gestattet. Die Kopiergebühren sind abgegolten. Alle Rechte vorbehalten.

Klett

GK + EK **10 Opposites**

Find the opposites. Look at the example.

old   real   stupid (2x)   full   legal

new _____   _____   _____   _____   _____

_____

11 Nouns and adjectives and verbs

Complete the grids with the missing words.

GK

noun		technology	
adjective	real		electric

noun				
verb	to report	to sleep	to rob	to switch

EK

noun	science			secret
adjective		real	electrical	

noun		description		report		
verb	to invent		to work		to think	to rob

GK + EK **12 People and jobs**

Find the words.

1. Somebody who works for an agency: _____

2. People see him/her if they've got a toothache: _____

3. A group of people who do something bad together: _____

4. A man and a woman or a girl and a boy who are together: _____

5. A group of people who work together on a plane/ship: _____

GK 6. Workers work for him or her: _____

EK 6. Somebody who controls planes when they land/take off: _____

7. Somebody who finds out about secret things: _____

8. Somebody who knows a lot and is very good at something: _____

 © Ernst Klett Verlag GmbH, Stuttgart 2008 | www.klett.de
Von dieser Druckvorlage ist die Vervielfältigung für den eigenen Unterrichtsgebrauch
gestattet. Die Kopiergebühren sind abgegolten. Alle Rechte vorbehalten.

Orange Line 4
ISBN 978-3-12-547544-1

GK **13 Guessing game**

Find the words.

1. CABLKTOU
2. TYCRAOF
3. SESALGS
4. PAMLS
5. IPNA
6. NEPUESSS
7. TACRTRO
8. TMTARPENA

9. | 1 | 2 | 3 | 4 | 5 | 6 | | 7 | 8 | 9 | 10 | 11 | 12 | 13 |

1. If there is no electricity, there is a ... .
2. It's a large building where they make things.
3. People wear them if they can't see well.
4. You switch them on in rooms if it's too dark to see.
5. If something hurts a lot, you feel a ... .
6. They bring it into a story or movie to make it more interesting.
7. They use it to plough fields.
8. It's the American English word for 'flat'.
9. You use it to operate e.g. the TV or the video player.

GK + EK **14 Everyday English: At a motel**

Complete the dialogue. Be polite.

Woman: Motel reception. Ms Winter speaking. What can I do for you?

You: _____

_____

_____

_____

Say who is speaking. Then tell Ms Winter what's wrong with the hairdryer/shower in your room.

Woman: I'm sorry to hear that. I'll do what I can. What's your room number, please?

You: _____

_____

Tell her your room number. Ask her to send someone up.

Woman: Of course, I will. I'll send you someone at once if that's OK with you.

You: _____

_____

Agree. Say something nice to her.

Woman: You're welcome. Can I do anything else for you?

You: _____

_____

Ask for something to eat and drink.

Woman: No problem. Right away.

You: _____

_____

Thank her and say goodbye.

Orange Line 4
ISBN 978-3-12-547544-1

© Ernst Klett Verlag GmbH, Stuttgart 2008 | www.klett.de
Von dieser Druckvorlage ist die Vervielfältigung für den eigenen Unterrichtsgebrauch
gestattet. Die Kopiergebühren sind abgegolten. Alle Rechte vorbehalten.

Klett

GK **15 Defrost¹ frozen² food or cook a meal?**

Write what you can do with a microwave and how you operate it. Write six sentences or more.
Look at the pictures and clues.

special bowls/
cups/plates

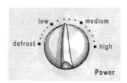

power

timer

Be careful!
➡ ... only special plates
➡ ... food/very hot
➡ ... not operate when empty

You can use a microwave to defrost frozen food.

_____

_____

_____

_____

_____

_____

¹to defrost [ˌdiːˈfrɒst] – *auftauen*, ²frozen [ˈfrəʊzn] – *gefroren*

EK **15 An alien story**

Continue the story. Write five sentences or more.

It's a beautiful night with a full moon and thousands of

stars in the sky. But Robert isn't happy. He hasn't finished

his alien story. He hasn't even written a single sentence.

Suddenly, there is a flare _____

_____

_____

_____

_____

_____

_____

_____

_____

 © Ernst Klett Verlag GmbH, Stuttgart 2008 | www.klett.de
Von dieser Druckvorlage ist die Vervielfältigung für den eigenen Unterrichtsgebrauch
gestattet. Die Kopiergebühren sind abgegolten. Alle Rechte vorbehalten.

Orange Line 4
ISBN 978-3-12-547544-1

GK + EK **16 Group work**

What do you say to your teacher/partner(s)? Be polite.

1. You want to work with a partner of your choice[1].

_____

2. You don't understand the task.

_____

3. You don't know what to do first.

_____

4. You don't understand the meaning of a word.

_____

5. Your idea is to make a poster with real photos.

_____

6. You tell the others that you'll take the photos and print them.

_____

[1]choice ['tʃɔɪs] – *Wahl*

EK **17 Mixed bag: Alf**

Complete the text with the missing words.

You know 'Alf', don't you? Alf's _____ name is Gordon Shumway and he is an alien.

One day his spaceship crashes[1] in the garage of the Tanner family. His spaceship hasn't broken

into pieces, but important things _____ damaged and he can't leave again. Gordon is

_____ 'ALF' by the Tanner family, which is short for 'Alien Life Form'. The Tanners don't

know what to do _____ their strange guest. Nobody must know about him.

So Alf _____ hidden in the kitchen and he _____ leave the house during the day.

Alf comes from the _____ 'Melmac', where he's part of the Melmac Spaceship Guard.

His job is to care for the _____ on his planet and to protect them from enemies. But

then _____ is a terrible war and Melmac finally explodes[2]. Melmac's green sky and its

blue grass don't _____ any longer. Alf is lucky. He isn't _____ because he's in his

_____ far away from Melmac. After days in space, Alf follows a signal to Earth. For weeks

the Tanners hope that the alien can _____ his spaceship and _____ them.

But Alf _____ his life on Earth. His _____ activities are watching TV, doing

nothing and eating. The alien has eight stomachs and is always _____. Alf's favourite food

is cats, and Lucky, the Tanner's cat, _____ be very careful.

[1]to crash [kræʃ] – *krachen*, [2]to explode [ɪk'spləʊd] – *explodieren*

Orange Line 4
ISBN 978-3-12-547544-1
© Ernst Klett Verlag GmbH, Stuttgart 2008 | www.klett.de
Von dieser Druckvorlage ist die Vervielfältigung für den eigenen Unterrichtsgebrauch
gestattet. Die Kopiergebühren sind abgegolten. Alle Rechte vorbehalten.

GK **18 Mediation and communication: Podcasts**

Situation: Ein polnischer Austauschschüler ist bei dir zu Gast und ihr bereitet gemeinsam eine Präsentation zu neuen Kommunikationsmöglichkeiten per Internet vor. Dein Gastschüler spricht nur wenig Englisch und kennt sich nicht mit Podcasting aus.

A **Podcast** is a digital media file[1], which you download from the Internet. Then you listen to and/or watch the podcast on a personal computer or on a portable media player. Podcasts are usually audio or video files and are often like radio or TV programmes. But they are not real-time. To download podcasts you need a personal computer with an Internet connection and a so-called aggregator. (This is the software.) If you want to watch or listen to a podcast on a portable media player (e.g. MP3 player), you'll need to copy the files.
A lot of podcasts are like private radio shows dealing with different everyday topics, from news to culture to entertainment. Others are like music programmes. Today newspapers and magazines even offer recorded programmes and some of their articles in audio form. Thus you can listen to an article and needn't read it. The German Chancellor, Angela Merkel, is one of the few politicians in the world who uses podcasts regularly to explain her political ideas to young people.

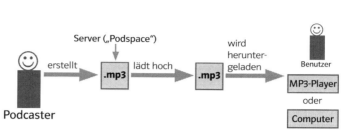

[1]file [faɪl] – *Datei*

Übertrage die wichtigsten Informationen für deinen Gastschüler ins Deutsche.

1. Was sind Podcasts?

_____

2. Wer kann Podcasts empfangen?

_____

3. Wie nutzt man sie?

_____

4. Welche Inhalte können Podcasts haben?

_____

EK **18 Mediation and communication: Podcasts**

Situation: Eine englische Schülerin ist bei dir zu Gast und ihr bereitet gemeinsam eine Präsentation zu neuen Kommunikationsmöglichkeiten per Internet vor.

a) *Ihr seid dabei zu klären, welche Technik ihr für eure Präsentation benötigt.*

☑ Laptop
☑ Beamer
☑ internetfähiges Handy
☑ MP3-Player
☑ Flip-Chart
☑ Stifte

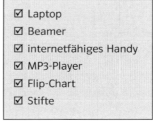

 © Ernst Klett Verlag GmbH, Stuttgart 2008 | www.klett.de
Von dieser Druckvorlage ist die Vervielfältigung für den eigenen Unterrichtsgebrauch gestattet. Die Kopiergebühren sind abgegolten. Alle Rechte vorbehalten.

Orange Line 4
ISBN 978-3-12-547544-1

Exchange pupil: Well, the laptop isn't a problem at all. We can use mine, if that's OK with you. But I don't understand 'Beamer'. A 'beam' is a long piece of wood you need to build houses or bridges or it's the light that comes from the lights of a car.

You: 'Beamer' is the German word for _____

_____

_____

Exchange pupil: Oh, I see. A data projector. And what is 'internetfähiges'? I mean, I understand 'Internet', but I cannot imagine what "fähiges" is. And 'Handy'? We use the word 'handy' for something that is useful.

You: _____

_____

_____

b) *Deine Gastschülerin kennt sich nicht mit Podcasting aus.*

Ein **Podcast** ist eine digitale Mediendatei[1], die man über das Internet herunterladen kann.
Podcasts sind in der Regel Audio- oder Videodateien und sie ähneln Rundfunk- oder Fernsehprogrammen. Um Podcasts nutzen zu können, braucht man einen Computer mit Internetzugang und eine

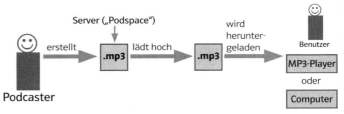

spezielle Software. Mittels USB-Kabel z.B. kann man die Audio- oder Videodateien dann auf MP3-Spieler oder Handy übertragen.
Viele Podcasts sind wie private Radiosendungen zu den unterschiedlichsten Themen. Andere wiederum ähneln Musikprogrammen. Zeitungen und Zeitschriften bieten neuerdings ausgewählte Artikel per Podcast vorgelesen an. So kann man einen Artikel „hören" anstatt zu lesen.
Die Bundeskanzlerin, Angela Merkel, ist eine der wenigen Politiker weltweit, die dieses Medium regelmäßig nutzen, um die Politik der Regierung zu erklären.

[1]*Mediendatei* – media file [faɪl]

Übertrage die wichtigsten Informationen für sie ins Englische.

1. What are podcasts?

_____

_____

2. Who can use podcasts?

_____

_____

3. What kind of files can podcasts be?

_____

_____

Orange Line 4
ISBN 978-3-12-547544-1
© Ernst Klett Verlag GmbH, Stuttgart 2008 | www.klett.de
Von dieser Druckvorlage ist die Vervielfältigung für den eigenen Unterrichtsgebrauch gestattet. Die Kopiergebühren sind abgegolten. Alle Rechte vorbehalten.

klett

Unit 4   Home and away

1 Let's listen: Our flight is delayed

GK + EK a) *Complete the text with the missing words.*

> *** AMERICAN AIRLINES *** We are sorry to say that our flight to Dallas, TX
>
> is _____ *** Planes can't _____
>
> Minneapolis Airport at the moment because of terrible _____ there ***

GK b) *Are the sentences right or wrong? Tick (✔).*

	right	wrong
1. Jim and Jane are feeling cold.		
2. They hope to get a flight on another plane.		
3. They want to call their parents to tell them about their problem.		
4. Jim would like to stay in LA over Thanksgiving.		
5. Jane would also like to spend Thanksgiving in LA.		
6. Jim thinks it is useless to wait and wants to go back to college.		

EK b) *Who is it? Tick (✔). Be careful: Two of the eight questions get two ticks.*

Who …	Jim	Jane	Martha
1. thinks that they should phone their parents?			
2. hopes that they must stay in LA over Thanksgiving?			
3. thinks that their mom would be unhappy if they stayed in LA?			
4. thinks it is useless to wait for their plane?			
5. isn't really interested in seeing old friends?			
6. will probably stay in LA alone over Thanksgiving?			
7. feels sorry for somebody who can't leave over Thanksgiving?			
8. suggests to ask their mom if they can invite a guest?			

GK c) *Tick (✔) the three right boxes.*

It is difficult for Jim and Jane's mom to believe that …

1. Jim and Jane's plane is delayed because of snow.
2. Jim and Jane want to go to Minneapolis because of the snow there.
3. it's very warm in LA.
4. they don't use another plane.
5. Jim and Jane want to go back to college.
6. Jim and Jane want to spend Thanksgiving with somebody else near LA.

© Ernst Klett Verlag GmbH, Stuttgart 2008 | www.klett.de
Von dieser Druckvorlage ist die Vervielfältigung für den eigenen Unterrichtsgebrauch
gestattet. Die Kopiergebühren sind abgegolten. Alle Rechte vorbehalten.

Orange Line 4
ISBN 978-3-12-547544-1

EK c) *Who is it? Tick (✔).*

Who finds it difficult to leave LA over Thanksgiving because …	Jim	Jane	Martha
1. there are problems with their flight?			
2. he/she loves somebody?			
3. there are money problems?			
4. his/her home country is too far away?			

GK d) *What is the result of the phone call to their mom? Tick (✔) the right box.*

Their mom …
1. wants to pay for some other tickets for Jim and Jane.
2. thinks it is too expensive to buy some other tickets.
3. thinks it is important that they are together in LA over Thanksgiving.

EK d) *What are the results of the phone call to their mom? Tick (✔) the right boxes.*

1. Their mom is ready to pay for …
a. some other tickets for Jim and Jane.
b. some other tickets for Jim and Jane, but she won't pay for Martha's ticket.
c. some other tickets for Jim, Jane and Martha.

2. Jim feels embarrassed because …
a. Martha may think that she is not rich enough for Jim's family.
b. he thinks his mother wants to check if Martha is good enough for him.
c. he wanted to keep it a secret that Martha is his new girlfriend.

GK e) *Which title matches the text best? Tick (✔) the right box.*

1. A very special flight
2. An expensive journey home for Thanksgiving
3. Thanksgiving away from home

EK e) *Which heading matches the text best? Tick (✔) the right box.*

1. How a delayed flight may be helpful to lovers[1]
2. A very special journey home
3. Getting together again for Thanksgiving

[1]lover ['lʌvə] – *Liebender/Liebende*

EK **2 Telling Martha about the good news**

Imagine you are Jim. Send Martha a short e-mail.

Write that
→ your mom wants to invite her to your home in Dallas,
→ your mom will pay for her flight.

Ask her in a friendly way to
♥ come with you,
(call you.

Finally, write
♥ something nice.

Hi Martha,

Orange Line 4
ISBN 978-3-12-547544-1

© Ernst Klett Verlag GmbH, Stuttgart 2008 | www.klett.de
Von dieser Druckvorlage ist die Vervielfältigung für den eigenen Unterrichtsgebrauch
gestattet. Die Kopiergebühren sind abgegolten. Alle Rechte vorbehalten.

Klett

GK + EK **3 Everyday English: Getting another flight to Dallas**

Imagine you are Jim. Complete the dialogue. Be polite.

You: _____

Ask for help. Tell them that you and your sister should be on the flight to Dallas which is delayed. But you need to get home.

Woman at desk: I'm sorry to hear that. I'll do what I can.

You: _____

Ask them for another flight to Dallas today.

Woman at desk: Let me see. There is a flight at 5:50 p.m., but there's only one seat left. There's just a small chance that there are some free seats on the night plane to Dallas.

You: _____

Ask when the plane leaves LA and arrives in Dallas.

EK Woman at desk: Let me see. There is a flight at 5:50 p.m. but there's only one seat left. And you need two, don't you?

You: _____

You need three seats because a friend is coming, too.

Woman at desk: Oh dear. I'm sorry, but I can't help you. We're fully booked[1]. There's just a little chance that there are some free seats on the night plane to Dallas.

You: _____

Ask when the plane leaves LA and arrives at Dallas.

Woman at desk: Just a minute. It leaves LA at 1:10 a.m. and arrives in Dallas at 6:00 a.m.

You: _____

Tell them that it's OK with you and ask for the price of a ticket.

Woman at desk: The price for each ticket is $264.00.

[1]fully booked [ˌfʊlɪ ˈbʊkt] – *total ausgebucht*

GK + EK **4 Let's read: Europeans on holiday**

Tourism[1] is a very important industry in many areas of Europe and there is a European office which does surveys about tourists and their holidays and works out the statistics. Some of the results are surprising and some are not.
First of all, the most important fact is that Europeans like their holidays. On average Europeans go on more than two holidays a year. The definition of a holiday here is a trip away from home for four days or more. Holidays are most popular with people from France[2] and Luxembourg; on average they have over 2.5 holidays a year. People from Greece and Ireland have the least[3] holidays; only 1.1 a year.   5

© Ernst Klett Verlag GmbH, Stuttgart 2008 | www.klett.de
Von dieser Druckvorlage ist die Vervielfältigung für den eigenen Unterrichtsgebrauch gestattet. Die Kopiergebühren sind abgegolten. Alle Rechte vorbehalten.

Orange Line 4
ISBN 978-3-12-547544-1

On average more Europeans go on holiday in their own country than go abroad, but there are big differences between countries. The results show that over 90% of the Greeks go on holiday in Greece, 88% of Spanish people stay in Spain[4] and 82% of the French stay in France. The UK and Germany were near the bottom of the list. 41% of the British stay in the UK and only 36% of all Germans stay in Germany.   10

Most Europeans go on holiday between July and September, but how do they travel? Most popular is by car and the second most popular is by plane. Again, there are big differences between countries.   15 Over 70% of the French and the Spanish go by car, but only 37% of the British go by car. In the UK air travel is most popular with over 50% of all people going on holiday by plane, but air travel is even more popular in Ireland; over 65% of people there go by plane. Over 53% of Germans go on holiday by car. The highest number of people who travel by boat are Greeks with over 20%. Trains are not popular at all. They are even less popular than bus holidays.   20

EK On average more Europeans organize their own holidays. Travel agents[5] have a hard life in Europe! Although, as you would expect, it's easier for them in countries where most people go abroad on holiday. In Sweden over 50% of holidays are organized by travel agents and in Germany it's about 31%. In Greece only 5% of all holidays are organized by travel agents and in France it's 11%. Of course, the Internet has made things even harder for travel agents. People can now find cheaper   25 holidays there.

GK [1]tourism ['tʊərɪzəm] – *Tourismus*, [2]France [frɑːns] – *Frankreich*, [3]least [liːst] – *wenigsten*, [4]Spain [speɪn] – *Spanien*
EK [1]tourism ['tʊərɪzəm] – *Tourismus*, [2]France [frɑːns] – *Frankreich*, [3]least [liːst] – *wenigsten*, [4]Spain [speɪn] – *Spanien*,
   [5]travel agents ['trævl ˌeɪdʒənts] – *Reisebüro*

GK + EK a) *Read the text. Find out about the average number of holidays that people in Europe have. Then write the names of the countries/continent next to the graph.*

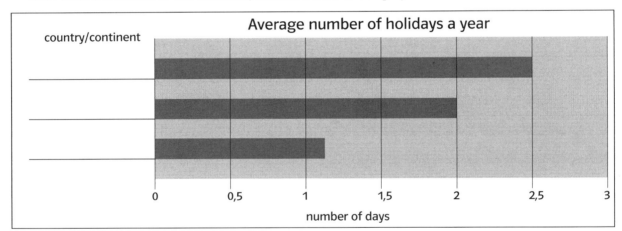

GK + EK b) *Find out about the different European nationalities and the number of people who like to spend their holidays in their own country. Then write the nationalities[1] and the percentage[2] next to and under the graph.*

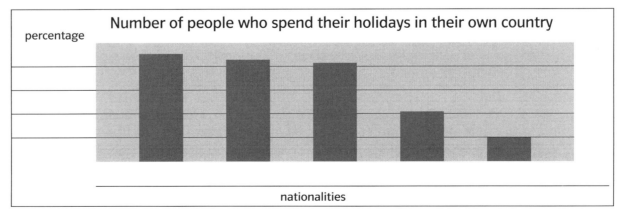

[1]nationality [ˌnæʃəˈnæləti] – *Nationalität*, [2]percentage [pəˈsentɪdʒ] – *Prozentwert*

Orange Line 4
ISBN 978-3-12-547544-1
© Ernst Klett Verlag GmbH, Stuttgart 2008 | www.klett.de
Von dieser Druckvorlage ist die Vervielfältigung für den eigenen Unterrichtsgebrauch gestattet. Die Kopiergebühren sind abgegolten. Alle Rechte vorbehalten.

GK c) *Show how the different European nationalities go on holiday. Fill in the percentage.*

nationality/ transport by	the French	the Spanish	the British	the Irish	the Germans	the Greek
car				–		–
plane	–	–			–	–
boat	–	–	–	–	–	

EK c) *Show how the different European nationalities go on holiday. Fill in the percentages.*
(Be careful. There are not percentages given for every field. Fill in "–" then.)

nationality/ transport by	the French	the Spanish	the British	the Irish	the Germans	the Greek
car						
plane						
boat						

GK + EK d) *Write down the forms of transport – from the most popular one to the least popular one.*

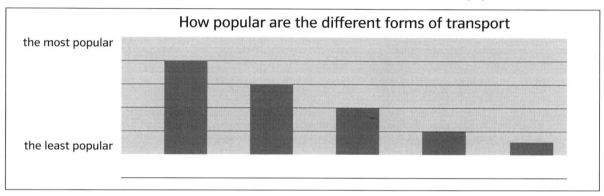

EK e) *Why do travel agents have a hard life in Europe?*

_____

_____

_____

GK **5 You help me and I'll help you**

Write three 'if'-clauses. Look at the clues.

3. repair your sister's bike ➡ she/help you with your homework

4. do the shopping

1. wash the car ➡ Dad/let you go to the disco

2. help Grandpa in the garden ➡ you/get some extra money from him

Mum/wash your dirty jeans ⬇

1. If you wash the car, Dad will let you go to the disco.

_____

_____

_____

_____

© Ernst Klett Verlag GmbH, Stuttgart 2008 | www.klett.de
Von dieser Druckvorlage ist die Vervielfältigung für den eigenen Unterrichtsgebrauch
gestattet. Die Kopiergebühren sind abgegolten. Alle Rechte vorbehalten.

Orange Line 4
ISBN 978-3-12-547544-1

GK **6 You don't help me and I won't help you**

Write three 'if'-clauses. Look at the clues.

| 1. not wash the car | ➡ | Dad/not let you go to the disco |
| 3. not clean your room | ➡ | you/not get your pocket money on Saturday |

| 2. not finish your homework | ➡ | Mum/not go to the shops with you |
| 4. not help Mum with the meal | ➡ | we/not be finished with dinner before the film starts |

1. If you don't wash the car, Dad won't let you go to the disco.

_____

_____

_____

GK **7 If he wins a lot of money**

a) *Complete the 'if'-clauses.*

If John __wins__ a lot of money, he __will buy__ a Porsche.

If he _____ a Porsche, he _____

lots of girls to go for a ride. If the girls _____ crazy

about him, he _____ great.

win/buy

have/invite

be

feel

If Jim __wins__ a lot of money, he __won't talk__ about it and

he _____ it on silly things, he'll save it all.

If he _____ anybody that he is rich,

he _____ give any money to others.

win/not talk

not spend

not tell

not have to

b) *What will you do if you win a lot of money? And what will you __not do__. Write three 'if'-clauses.*

If I _____

_____

_____

_____

_____

_____

Orange Line 4
ISBN 978-3-12-547544-1
© Ernst Klett Verlag GmbH, Stuttgart 2008 | www.klett.de
Von dieser Druckvorlage ist die Vervielfältigung für den eigenen Unterrichtsgebrauch
gestattet. Die Kopiergebühren sind abgegolten. Alle Rechte vorbehalten.

Klett

GK **8 A questionnaire: "What will you do if . . .?"**

Write four questions for a questionnaire about money. Use 'if'-clauses.

1. ~~what/do - if/suddenly get a lot of money~~
2. where/go on holiday – if/have enough money
3. what/buy – if/money/ be no problem
4. how much money/give to others – if/win in a lottery
5. how much money/ save – if/get more money than you can spend

1. What will you do if you suddenly get a lot of money?

_____

_____

_____

_____

EK **5 Promises and warnings**

a) *What do you promise? Use conditional clauses Type I.*

| wash the car | help you in the garden | repair your bike for you | do the shopping |

1. You want to go to disco.
2. You need some extra money.

1. Dad, if you let me go to the disco, I'll wash the car.

2. Grandpa, _____

_____

3. You need help with your homework.

3. Hey sis, _____

_____

4. You want to wear your best jeans. They're dirty.

4. Mum, _____

_____

b) *What do your parents, brother or sister say? Use conditional clauses Type I.*

| go to the disco | go to the shops with you | let you use it again | lend you my clothes again |

1. You haven't washed the car.
2. You haven't finished your homework.

1. If you don't wash the car, we won't let you go to the disco.

2. _____

_____

3. You've used your brother's bike. It's broken.

3. _____

_____

4. You've worn your sister's T-shirt. It's dirty.

4. _____

_____

 © Ernst Klett Verlag GmbH, Stuttgart 2008 | www.klett.de
Von dieser Druckvorlage ist die Vervielfältigung für den eigenen Unterrichtsgebrauch gestattet. Die Kopiergebühren sind abgegolten. Alle Rechte vorbehalten.

Orange Line 4
ISBN 978-3-12-547544-1

EK **6 Hansel and Gretel in the forest**

Hansel and Gretel tell each other about the dangers¹ in the forest. Complete their dialogue. Use conditional clauses Type I.

birds eat up all the breadcrumbs²	→	get lost in the forest	eat from the sweets on the house	→ be in trouble

get fat³ from all the food → the old woman/eat you

Gretel: Hansel, what will happen if the birds eat up all the breadcrumbs?

Hansel: If they eat up all the _____

Gretel: Hansel, what will happen _____

Hansel: If we _____

_____

Gretel, what will happen _____

Gretel: If you _____

_____

¹danger [ˈdeɪndʒə] – *Gefahr,* ²breadcrumb [ˈbredkrʌm] – *Brotkrume,* ³fat [fæt] – *fett*

EK **7 If he won a lot of money**

a) *Complete the sentences. Use conditional clauses Type II.*

If John __won__ a lot of money, he __would buy__ a Porsche.

If he _____ a Porsche, he _____

lots of girls to go for a ride and they _____ like

mad to meet him. He _____ great if lots of

girls _____ crazy about him.

win/buy

have/invite

be

feel

be

If Jim __won__ a lot of money, he __wouldn't talk__ about it and

he _____ it on silly things, he'd save it all.

If he _____ anybody that he was rich,

he _____ the money with others.

win/not talk

not spend

not tell

not have to share

Orange Line 4
ISBN 978-3-12-547544-1

© Ernst Klett Verlag GmbH, Stuttgart 2008 | www.klett.de
Von dieser Druckvorlage ist die Vervielfältigung für den eigenen Unterrichtsgebrauch
gestattet. Die Kopiergebühren sind abgegolten. Alle Rechte vorbehalten.

Klett

b) *What would <u>you</u> do if you won a lot of money? And what would you not do.*
   Write three conditional clauses Type II.

_____

_____

_____

_____

EK **8 A questionnaire: "What would you do if you were rich?"**

Write four questions for a questionnaire about money. Use conditional clauses Type II.

1. where/go on holiday – if/have enough money	1. Where would you go on holiday if _____
2. what/buy – if/money/ be no problem	2. _____
3. how much money/ give to others – if/ win in a lottery	3. _____
4. how much money/ save – if/get more money than you could spend	4. _____

EK **9 Survey: "What would you do if you suddenly got rich?"**

In a TV show students were asked that question. This is what they answered.
Write a factual text. Write five sentences or more.

Topic of survey:
What would you do if you suddenly got rich?
Survey group:
8–9th Grade, high school, California
Number: 25

	boys	girls
have a big party	93%	88%
save and think of the future	84%	91%
buy expensive clothes	35%	72%
give part of the money to poor peple	51%	52%

These statistics are from a survey of 25 _____

_____

_____

_____

_____

_____

_____

© Ernst Klett Verlag GmbH, Stuttgart 2008 | www.klett.de
Von dieser Druckvorlage ist die Vervielfältigung für den eigenen Unterrichtsgebrauch
gestattet. Die Kopiergebühren sind abgegolten. Alle Rechte vorbehalten.

Orange Line 4
ISBN 978-3-12-547544-1

EK **10 If I were . . .**

Choose one of the following three "roles" or find another "role". Write what you would/could do if you were a/an . . . . Write four sentences or more.

If I were an alien . . .	If I were an angel . . .	If I were a famous star . . .	If I were ??? . . .

_____

_____

_____

_____

_____

GK **11 Trucker words**

Do the puzzle and find the words.

Down ⇩
1. You need it to drive a car or truck. (2 words)
3. a place where you can have a snack
5. what trucks carry
8. a place where you can have a break during a trip (2 words)
9. what truckers do with the goods

Across ⇨
2. AE word for a road between states
4. type of a road (AE)
6. You leave a motorway at the ... .
7. You do it at borders, in streets, etc.
9. what a trucker drives
10. When a car or truck does not work it has a ... .
11. the line between one country/ state and another

Orange Line 4
ISBN 978-3-12-547544-1

© Ernst Klett Verlag GmbH, Stuttgart 2008 | www.klett.de
Von dieser Druckvorlage ist die Vervielfältigung für den eigenen Unterrichtsgebrauch
gestattet. Die Kopiergebühren sind abgegolten. Alle Rechte vorbehalten.

EK **11 Trucker words**

Do the puzzle and find the words.

Down ⇩
1. BE word for Interstate
3. Truckers often give it to people who want to travel cheaply.
4. a place where you can have a snack
5. what truckers do with the goods
8. AE word for toilet
9. AE word for motorway
13. a place where you can have a break during a trip (2 words)
16. You do it at borders, in streets etc.

Across ⇨
2. what trucks carry
6. When a car or truck does not work, it has a … .
7. what a trucker drives
10. 1,000 kg are a … .
11. the line between one country/ state and another
12. You leave a motorway at the … .
14. the place where you can park your car (2 words)
15. A trucker should also be a good … .
17. You need it to drive a car or truck. (2 words)

GK **12 Vacations on a ranch**

Find the words. Look at the clues.

no a nahre   byosowc   tactel   lilhs   oycnnsa   ytsdu   a reicampf

tactel ridev   porgni   sehrocabk gnidir   idryt

qeursa naced

a roode

The place where you stay: on a ranch

The people who work there: _____

Animals there: _____

The scenery that you often find there: _____ _____

There it can be: _____ _____

What you can have, can do or learn to do …   _____ _____ _____

_____ _____

What you can visit: _____

 Klett

© Ernst Klett Verlag GmbH, Stuttgart 2008 | www.klett.de
Von dieser Druckvorlage ist die Vervielfältigung für den eigenen Unterrichtsgebrauch
gestattet. Die Kopiergebühren sind abgegolten. Alle Rechte vorbehalten.

Orange Line 4
ISBN 978-3-12-547544-1

EK **12 Vacations in the wild west**

Find the words. Look at the clues.

pcma   nahrc   parsecm   byosowc   sesrocluon   cianb   a restof

reogg   germvleihonw   nartifg   reicampf   roode   sue bwo dan rowra

niigks

The places where you can stay: _____ _____

The people who come or work there: _____ _____ _____

What you often live in: _____

The scenery that you often find there: _____ _____

How the scenery can be: _____

What you can do/have/go to … in the summer and in the winter: _____ _____ _____

_____ _____

13 Verbs

Match the verbs with the best words or phrases.

EK   in Mexico   a border   a cattle drive   on a journey   a ranch   tourists   very long   a car

to attract _____   to join _____

to cross _____   to own _____

to end up _in Mexico_____   to set off _____

to last _____   to spray _____

EK   a meal   a track or a bird   a secret   a border   tourists   one's best friend

in prison   a play   on a journey   a car   something frozen   very long

to attract _____   to miss _____

to cross _____   to produce _____

to discover _____   to serve _____

to end up _____   to set off _____

to identify _____   to spray _____

to last _____   to thaw _____

Orange Line 4
ISBN 978-3-12-547544-1
© Ernst Klett Verlag GmbH, Stuttgart 2008 | www.klett.de
Von dieser Druckvorlage ist die Vervielfältigung für den eigenen Unterrichtsgebrauch
gestattet. Die Kopiergebühren sind abgegolten. Alle Rechte vorbehalten.

14 Using adjectives

Find a good noun each.

GK 1. It can be dusty:

_____

2. It can be comfortable:

_____

3. It can be delayed:

_____

4. You can be stranded there:

_____

EK 1. It can be vast:

_____

2. It can be comfortable:

_____

3. It is often all inclusive:

_____

4. You can be stranded there:

_____

5. You can have it over easy or sunny side up:

_____

GK ## 15 Mixed bag: About the life of a trucker in the US

Complete the text with the right words from the box.

| traffic | goods | driver's license | comfortable | have | scenery | sights |
| won't | first of all | rest areas | Interstates | miss | a breakdown |

How much do truckers get?

In the US, they usually pay truckers by the mile.
A trucker has to drive as many miles as he or she can to get good money. So it's easy to understand that US drivers like

long-distance tours on the _____ best. But it is

one thing to transport the _____ from one place to

another: But what about the hours of waiting because of _____ jams? And what about

repair times because the truck has a _____? It's difficult to say how much money
a trucker brings home, but it's about $300 to $1,200 a week.

At what age can you become a trucker?

_____ of all, you need a _____, of course. In the US, you can get it

from age 16. If you want to drive a truck across the US, you _____ to be 21 years old.

But most companies _____ give you a job if you are not 23+ or even 25+!

The good & the bad things about a trucker's life

☺ You travel and see all the famous

_____ and some dramatic

_____. You have lots of breaks and

meet lots of truckers in the _____.

☹ It's not _____ to sleep in a

truck. It's hard to be on the road all the time

and you _____ your family and

friends.

 © Ernst Klett Verlag GmbH, Stuttgart 2008 | www.klett.de
Von dieser Druckvorlage ist die Vervielfältigung für den eigenen Unterrichtsgebrauch
gestattet. Die Kopiergebühren sind abgegolten. Alle Rechte vorbehalten.

Orange Line 4
ISBN 978-3-12-547544-1

EK **15 Mixed bag: About the life of a trucker in the US**

Complete the text with the missing words.

How much are truckers paid?

In the US, a trucker _____ usually paid by the mile. A trucker has

to drive _____ many miles as he can to get good money. It is easy

to understand that US drivers like long-distance tours on the

_____ best. But it's one thing to transport the _____ from one place to another:

But what about the hours of waiting because of _____ jams? And what about repair times

_____ the truck has a _____? It's difficult to say how _____ money a

driver brings home, but it's about $300 _____ $1,200 a week.

At what age can you become a trucker?

_____ of all, you need a _____, of course. In the US, you can get it

_____ age 16. If you want to drive a truck across the US, you have _____ be

21 years old. But most firms _____ give you a job if you are not 23+ or even 25+!

The good & the bad about trucking

☺ You travel and see all the famous

_____ and some overwhelming

_____. You have lots of breaks and meet

loads of truckers in the _____.

☹ It's not _____ to sleep

in a truck. It's hard to be on the road all the

time and you _____ your family and

friends.

GK **16 A survey**

In a TV show they asked truckers about their job. Here are some of the good points which they gave. Write a factual text. Write five sentences or more.

Topic of survey:
What is good and what is bad about
a trucker's life?
Survey group: truckers from age 28–54
Number: 20

good	
to travel and see a lot	93%
to have a lot of breaks and meet other truckers	84%
no boss to look over your shoulder	51%
not need to work together with others	35%

This was a survey about what is good and what
is bad about a trucker's life.

_____

_____

_____

_____

_____

Orange Line 4
ISBN 978-3-12-547544-1
© Ernst Klett Verlag GmbH, Stuttgart 2008 | www.klett.de
Von dieser Druckvorlage ist die Vervielfältigung für den eigenen Unterrichtsgebrauch
gestattet. Die Kopiergebühren sind abgegolten. Alle Rechte vorbehalten.

Klett

GK + EK **17 Mediation and communication: US road signs**

Situation: Deine Großeltern bereiten sich auf ihre US-Reise vor und wollen für einzelne Touren auch ein Auto mieten. Im Internet sind sie bei der Suche nach US-Verkehrszeichen auf folgende gestoßen. Hilf ihnen die Schilder zu verstehen.

1.

4.

2.

3.

5.

ex·cept [ɪk'sept] I. *transitives Verb* 1. ausnehmen, ausschließen (from aus) II. *Präposition* außer, ausgenommen; ***except for*** bis auf, mit Ausnahme	tran·sit ['trænsɪt] I. *Substantiv* 1. Durchgang; 2. Transit-, Durchgangsverkehr; 3. Transport	tune [tjuːn] I. *transitives Verb* 1. *(Musikinstrument)* stimmen; 2. *(Radio)* einstellen; 3. *(Motor)* tunen	per·mit ['pɜːmɪt] I. *Substantiv* 1. Erlaubnis; 2. Genehmigung, Bewilligung; 3. Passierschein, Ausweis

Erkläre ihnen kurz und knapp die Aussage der einzelnen Schilder.

_____

_____

_____

_____

_____

_____

© Ernst Klett Verlag GmbH, Stuttgart 2008 | www.klett.de
Von dieser Druckvorlage ist die Vervielfältigung für den eigenen Unterrichtsgebrauch gestattet. Die Kopiergebühren sind abgegolten. Alle Rechte vorbehalten.

Orange Line 4
ISBN 978-3-12-547544-1

Unit 5   Stars in your eyes?

◎ 1 Let's listen: Summer films

GK a) *What about David and what about Glenda? Tick (✔) the right boxes.*

	David			Glenda		
	likes	has no idea/ has never done it, but is interested in	does not like	likes	has no idea/ has never done it, but is interested in	does not like
1. a dark movie theater in the summer						
2. watching a movie outside						
3. the new Simpsons' movie						
4. the new Harry Potter movie						
5. the last few Harry Potter movies						
6. comedies						

b) *Who is it? Tick (✔).*

Who …	David	Glenda
1. is only little interested in movies?		
2. is interested in different types of movies?		
3. likes The Simpsons' movie better than The Simpsons' series?		
4. knows something about the Harry Potter books and movies?		
5. loves one of the actresses in the Harry Potter movies?		
6. thinks that the last few Harry Potter movies were too scary?		
7. thinks that Harry Potter movies are for kids?		
8. likes comedies?		
9. thinks you can go to the cinema in rainy weather?		

c) *Which sentence is the best summary of the text? Tick (✔) the right box.*

1. David and Linda are talking about the movies which they both like best. ☐

2. David and Linda are having an argument about Harry Potter movies. ☐

3. David is trying to show Linda that watching movies can be fun in the summer, too. ☐

EK a) *What about David and what about Glenda? Tick (✔) the right boxes.*

	David			Glenda		
	likes	has no idea/ has never done it, but is interested in	does not like	likes	has no idea/ has never done it, but is interested in	does not like
1. a dark movie theater in the summer						
2. watching a movie outside						
3. the new Simpsons' movie						
4. Charlie Chaplin movies						
5. movies without sound						
6. the new Harry Potter movie						
7. the last few Harry Potter movies						
8. comedies						

Orange Line 4
ISBN 978-3-12-547544-1

© Ernst Klett Verlag GmbH, Stuttgart 2008 | www.klett.de
Von dieser Druckvorlage ist die Vervielfältigung für den eigenen Unterrichtsgebrauch
gestattet. Die Kopiergebühren sind abgegolten. Alle Rechte vorbehalten.

b) *What is true for David? Tick (✔) the three right boxes.*

David …
1. is only interested in funny movies.
2. is interested in different types of movies.
3. knows something about very old movies.
4. knows a lot about the different types of movies from comedies to love stories.
5. loves the actors and actresses who are in the Harry Potter movies.
6. loves one of the actresses in the Harry Potter movies.

c) *What is true for Glenda? Tick (✔) the three right boxes.*

Glenda …
1. is only a little interested in movies.
2. is very interested in fantasy movies.
3. knows a lot about the Harry Potter movies.
4. only knows a little about movies.
5. thinks going to the cinema is something you can do in rainy weather.
6. thinks going to the cinema is an autumn or a winter activity.

d) *Which sentence gives the best summary of the text? Tick (✔) the right box.*

1. David and Linda are talking about the movies which they both like best.
2. David and Linda are having an argument about Harry Potter films.
3. David is trying to convince Linda that watching movies can be fun in the summer, too.

2 Let's read: A letter about the Oscars

GK+EK

1382 West Boulevard
Los Angeles, CA 90124
Saturday, March 1st

Dear Emma,

You'll never believe this but I went to the Oscars last week with Graham. I still can't believe it myself.
It was so strange. You know that I'm staying in Los Angeles for the summer with some friends who
I met on holiday last year, don't you? Well, Graham, my friend from college, called
me last week and asked me to go to the Oscars with him. He was nominated[1] for
the award 'Best Young Cameraman' on a short, foreign film or something like that. 5
Did you know?
Well, he only just had enough money for himself to fly to Los Angeles and none
of his friends had enough money to go with him. He didn't want to go alone and
he knew I was in LA, so that's why he asked me to go with him. I almost didn't go 10
either because I didn't have anything to wear. Well, you can't go in jeans and
a T-shirt or anything like that, can you? And of course, I didn't take any dresses
with me to LA – I don't even have an evening dress. But luckily a friend's sister
lent me a dress.
And I'm glad I went! At the beginning it was really scary because we had to walk 15
in on the red carpet with all those photographers around who had their cameras
pointed at us. But after that it was great. It was so interesting watching these
people you've only seen on TV or in the cinema. A lot of them don't look the same
as on TV. They don't look real. They've got so much make-up on that they look
plastic[2] – yes, even the men. And they smile all the time. I thought their smiles 20
were painted on. And their clothes! You've never seen so many glamorous clothes
in one place. I don't know how some of the women could walk in their dresses.
And most of the dresses were backless or low-cut – or backless and low-cut!
And I saw lots of really famous people but I'm terrible at names so I've forgotten them all again.
I know that I saw Brad Pitt. Oh, he's so attractive. He's even more attractive in real life than in the 25
films. I wanted to go and kiss him. No, don't worry. I didn't.

 © Ernst Klett Verlag GmbH, Stuttgart 2008 | www.klett.de
Von dieser Druckvorlage ist die Vervielfältigung für den eigenen Unterrichtsgebrauch
gestattet. Die Kopiergebühren sind abgegolten. Alle Rechte vorbehalten.

Orange Line 4
ISBN 978-3-12-547544-1

EK | Graham is going home again tomorrow, but we've had a great week while he's been here. While we were at the Academy Awards, we were invited to a few parties. Don't get excited, there was nobody famous there but they were still great. It was so funny because we're staying in this tiny student flat where nobody cares much about clothes. And even if they do, they don't have any money. Then in the evenings we went to parties where people all wore really glamorous clothes and everyone hoped that a famous director would be there or something. In fact, there was a famous director at one party. But no, I wasn't offered a part in a film! | 30

GK+EK | Oh, I've got lots more news for you but I have to go now. I'm meeting a new friend at a restaurant. I'll tell you who it is when I get home. | 35

Love, Helen

¹to nominate ['nɒmɪneɪt] – *nominieren*, ²plastic ['plæstɪk] – *Plastik*

GK+EK a) *Read the text and complete the sentences.*

Helen was so lucky to go to the Oscars with Graham because …

👍 she was staying in Los Angeles at the time of the Oscars.

👍 Graham invited her _____

👍 Graham didn't _____ to pay

for any flights for his friends from home.

👍 Graham didn't _____ , but

wanted to have somebody at his side.

👍 Graham knew that Helen _____

It was bad luck that …

👎 Graham's friends couldn't come because _____

👎 Helen hadn't taken _____

GK+EK b) *Find the right endings to the eight sentences. Draw lines.*

| 1. First Helen felt scared because of … |
| 2. Later she felt OK because … |
| 3. Helen thought that a lot of stars there didn't … |
| 4. She didn't like the fact that most stars, even the men, … |
| 5. Helen felt that the smile on the faces of the stars all night long … |
| 6. She found it difficult to understand how … |
| 7. Most of the women's dresses … |
| 8. Helen was surprised how more attractive … |

| A) look the same as on TV. |
| B) was unreal. |
| C) some of the women could move in their dresses. |
| D) Brad Pitt looked in real life than on the screen. |
| E) were sexy. |
| F) the media crowd. |
| G) she enjoyed watching all those stars. |
| H) wore so much make-up. |

Orange Line 4
ISBN 978-3-12-547544-1
© Ernst Klett Verlag GmbH, Stuttgart 2008 | www.klett.de
Von dieser Druckvorlage ist die Vervielfältigung für den eigenen Unterrichtsgebrauch gestattet. Die Kopiergebühren sind abgegolten. Alle Rechte vorbehalten.

EK c) *Explain what difference Helen found between everyday life and the world of the stars. Answer in sentences.*

_____

_____

_____

GK **3 The Hollywood Walk of Fame**

Complete the sentences with the right relative pronoun. Use 'who' or 'which'.

Have you ever heard of the Hollywood Walk of Fame? It's a sidewalk in Los Angeles _____ runs along Hollywood Boulevard and Vine Street. Most tourists _____ visit the city want to see it. In 1958 the city asked some Californian artists[1] to make the place more attractive to tourists. But none of the suggestions _____ the artists made were really big hits. Then Oliver Weismuller had a great idea. He wanted to fix thousands of stars in a sidewalk. Weissmuller's project, _____ wasn't too expensive, found the city's interest at once. Hollywood Boulevard, _____ they finally chose as the best place for the project, became the Hollywood Walk of Fame. During the next months they fixed 2,500 stars in the ground there. On February 9, 1960, they gave the first star to Joanne Woodward, _____ was a very famous actress at that time. She was married to the actor and director Paul Newman, _____ got his star on the Walk of Fame some time later. Within the next 16 months, they filled 1,558 stars with the names of famous people _____ had done something great in the fields of motion pictures, radio, television and other areas.

[1]artist ['ɑːtɪst] – *Künstler/in*

GK **4 The four stolen stars**

Make sentences. Use the right relative pronoun 'who' or 'which'. Look at the example.

1. The first two stars	who / which	lost their stars were James Stewart and Kirk Douglas.
2. The third star	who / which	was stolen was for Gene Autry.
3. The person	who / which	stole it lived in Iowa.
4. Gene Autry was the only star	who / which	got five stars on the Hollywood Walk of Fame.
5. Gregory Peck was the next star	who / which	lost his star.
6. His star is the only one	who / which	they never found.

 © Ernst Klett Verlag GmbH, Stuttgart 2008 | www.klett.de
Von dieser Druckvorlage ist die Vervielfältigung für den eigenen Unterrichtsgebrauch gestattet. Die Kopiergebühren sind abgegolten. Alle Rechte vorbehalten.

Orange Line 4
ISBN 978-3-12-547544-1

1. The first two stars who lost their stars were James Stewart and Kirk Douglas.

_____

_____

_____

_____

_____

_____

_____

_____

GK **5 Do you know it?**

Write four more sentences. Use the relative pronouns 'who' or 'which' and the information in the boxes. Look at the example.

~~"We are the champions"~~ ♣   J.K. Rowling ♥   Will Smith ♠   "Titanic" ♦   Ericsson *

first mobile phones *   James Cameron ♦   the Harry Potter books ♥   ~~the "Queen"~~ ♣   role of Robert Neville in "I am legend" ♠

make *   play ♠   produce ♦   ~~sing~~ ♣   write ♥

"We are the champions" is a song which Queen sang.

J. K. Rowling is the _____

_____

_____

_____

EK **3 The Hollywood Walk of Fame**

Complete the sentences. Use the passive simple past.

The Hollywood Walk of Fame is a sidewalk along Hollywood Boulevard and Vine Street in

Hollywood, Los Angeles. It is one of the city's most visited tourist attractions. It _____

_____ *(to design)* by Oliver Weismuller in 1958. In the late 1950s some Californian

artists[1] _____ *(to ask)* for their ideas of how to make the city more attractive

to tourists. But the suggestions that _____ *(to make)* by them were not really

big hits. Then the artist Oliver Weismuller had a great idea.

Orange Line 4
ISBN 978-3-12-547544-1
© Ernst Klett Verlag GmbH, Stuttgart 2008 | www.klett.de
Von dieser Druckvorlage ist die Vervielfältigung für den eigenen Unterrichtsgebrauch
gestattet. Die Kopiergebühren sind abgegolten. Alle Rechte vorbehalten.

His idea of thousands of stars in a sidewalk

_____ (to receive) with open arms
from the start and the Hollywood Walk of Fame

_____ (to be born).

Hollywood Boulevard _____ (to choose)

as the best place and 2,500 stars _____

_____ (to fix) in the ground there. On February 9, 1960, the first star

_____ (to give) to Joanne Woodward, a very famous actress at that time.

Within the next 16 months, 1,558 stars _____ (to fill) with the names of
famous people. Since then, about two stars a month are given to famous people.   ¹artist ['ɑːtɪst] – *Künstler*

EK **4 Tourists on Hollywood Walk of Fame**

Complete the tourist's questions. Use the passive simple past. Look at the clues.

Guide: Well, we had the las theft¹ of a star in November 2005.

Tourist: _____ whose star/
to steal

Guide: It was Gregory Peck's star.

Tourist: _____ how many
stars/
_____ before that one? to steal

Guide: Let me see. Three, I think.

Tourist: I mean, it's not easy to take a star out of the sidewalk, is it? how/stars/
to remove

_____

Guide: As far as I know they were taken away while they were repairing part of
the sidewalk.

Tourist: _____ missing stars/
to find

Guide: Yes, those ones were. But Gregory Peck's star still hasn't been found.

Tourist: _____ when/Gregory
Peck's star/to
Guide: In September 2006. replace

Tourist: _____ thieves² of the
other three
Guide: Yes, they were. Police finally caught them. stars/to catch

Tourist: _____ I mean why/the stars/
to take
who wants to have such a big and heavy stone in his home.

¹theft [θeft] – *Diebstahl*, ²thief [θiːf] – *Dieb*

 © Ernst Klett Verlag GmbH, Stuttgart 2008 | www.klett.de
Von dieser Druckvorlage ist die Vervielfältigung für den eigenen Unterrichtsgebrauch
gestattet. Die Kopiergebühren sind abgegolten. Alle Rechte vorbehalten.

Orange Line 4
ISBN 978-3-12-547544-1

EK **5 Hollywood's Walk of Fame categories**

Write six sentences. Use the verbs in the boxes in the passive simple past.
Use their negative and positive forms. Look at the clues and the example.

to be given   to be presented with   to be awarded with

Hollywood's Walk of Fame categories:					
	motion pictures	television	recording	radio	live performance

	wrong	right
the Beatles		
Kermit and The Simpsons		
Bugs Bunny		
Michael Jackson		

The Beatles weren't awarded with a star in the radio category. They were awarded with a star in the recording category.

EK **6 A quiz: Who was it done by?**

a) *Write four more questions for a quiz. Use the verbs in the boxes in the passive simple past.*
Look at the example. Always begin with 'Who was …' or 'Who were …'.

make   play   produce   sing   write

song "We are the champions" ♣   movie "Titanic" ♦   role of Robert Neville in "I am legend" ♠   first mobile phones *   the Harry Potter books ♥

Who was the song "We are the champions" sung by?

Orange Line 4
ISBN 978-3-12-547544-1
© Ernst Klett Verlag GmbH, Stuttgart 2008 | www.klett.de
Von dieser Druckvorlage ist die Vervielfältigung für den eigenen Unterrichtsgebrauch gestattet. Die Kopiergebühren sind abgegolten. Alle Rechte vorbehalten.

b) *Answer the five questions in sentences. Use the passive simple past.*

| Ericsson * | James Cameron ♦ | J.K. Rowling ♥ | the "Queen" ♣ | Will Smith ♠ |

_____

_____

_____

_____

_____

7 Mixed bag: Oscar words

Complete the text with the missing "Oscar" words.

GK

The Academy Awards or "the Oscars" is a _____ at which they give Oscars to the best directors, actors and writers[1]. The Oscar is a little _____ (only about 34 cm tall) and made of gold. On Awards night the stars and guests arrive in big and expensive _____ before they walk up the red _____. There they usually stop to _____ for the cameras. The women mostly wear _____ and sexy _____ _____, which are often _____ or _____.

EK The Academy Awards is a _____ at which the best directors, actors and writers[1] are given Oscars. The Oscar, whose official name is Academy Award, is a _____ which every famous actor or actress hopes to get once in a lifetime[2]. The Oscar is a little

_____ (only about 34 cm tall) and made of gold. The Awards night is a spectacular media event and the _____ and the TV report about it. On the Awards night the stars and guests arrive in big and expensive _____ before they walk up the red _____. There they hope to get the _____ of the photographers and camera men and they usually stop to _____ for the cameras. The women mostly wear _____ and sexy _____ _____ which are often _____ or _____.

[1]writer ['raɪtə] – *Schriftsteller/in*, [2]lifetime ['laɪftaɪm] – *Leben*

 © Ernst Klett Verlag GmbH, Stuttgart 2008 | www.klett.de
Von dieser Druckvorlage ist die Vervielfältigung für den eigenen Unterrichtsgebrauch
gestattet. Die Kopiergebühren sind abgegolten. Alle Rechte vorbehalten.

Orange Line 4
ISBN 978-3-12-547544-1

8 Music words

Complete the mind map.

GK

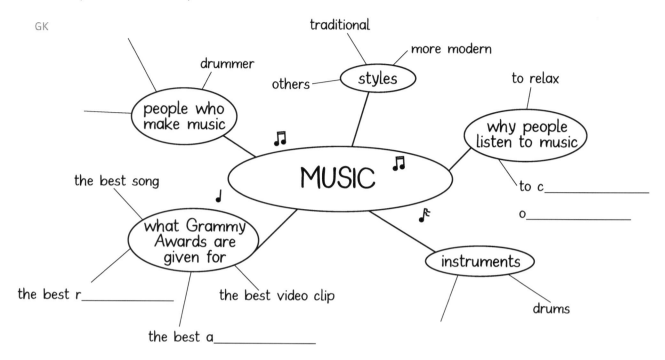

EK

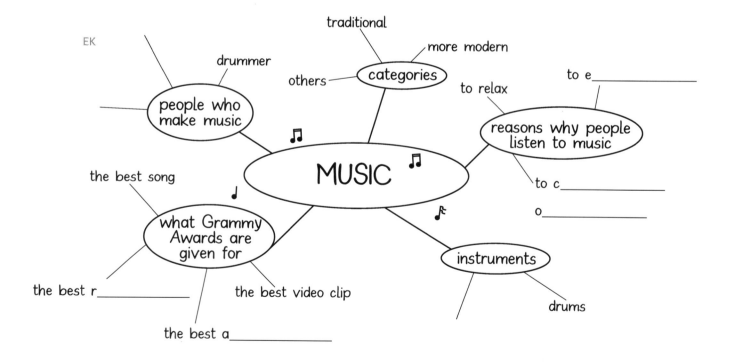

Orange Line 4
ISBN 978-3-12-547544-1

© Ernst Klett Verlag GmbH, Stuttgart 2008 | www.klett.de
Von dieser Druckvorlage ist die Vervielfältigung für den eigenen Unterrichtsgebrauch
gestattet. Die Kopiergebühren sind abgegolten. Alle Rechte vorbehalten.

9 Verbs and nouns

Complete the table with the missing verbs or nouns.

GK

verb	noun
to rock	
to invent	
to move	
to produce	
to record	

verb	noun
to rise	
	director
to rap	
	supporter
	view

EK

verb	noun
to battle	
to design	
to move	
to produce	

verb	noun
to rise	
to rap	
	supporter
	view

10 Using verbs

Find a good noun each. Look at the scrambled clues for some ideas.

GK

a rodcer   a milf   tiwh cimus   a etlter   ni a mufro

nechmapag   a rknid   a ltis   a dfrine   lod tisme

1. What you can produce: _____

2. What you can direct: _____

3. How you can chill out: _____

4. What you can post: _____

5. Where you can register: _____

6. What you can pop: _____

7. What you can sip: _____

8. What you can view: _____

9. Who you can support: _____

10. What you can reminisce over: _____

EK

na e-laim daesrds   a tnsigr   tusseg   ni a mufro   a rknid   a etlter

a nbda   a lcbu   a boko   a masgsee   a tema   lod tisme

1. What you can set up: _____

2. What you can attach: _____

3. What you can publish: _____

4. What you can receive: _____

5. Where you can register: _____

6. What you can post: _____

7. What you can form: _____

8. What you can join: _____

9. Who you can entertain: _____

10. Who you can beat: _____

11. What you can sip: _____

12. What you can reminisce over: _____

© Ernst Klett Verlag GmbH, Stuttgart 2008 | www.klett.de
Von dieser Druckvorlage ist die Vervielfältigung für den eigenen Unterrichtsgebrauch gestattet. Die Kopiergebühren sind abgegolten. Alle Rechte vorbehalten.

Orange Line 4
ISBN 978-3-12-547544-1

11 Adjectives in use

Match the adjectives with the word groups. Try to find the best word groups.

GK | glamorous | raw | outrageous | pristine | historical | red |

a _____ building a _____ hotel room

a _____ carpet a _____ piece of metal

a(n) _____ hairstyle a _____ evening dress

EK | complex | historical | flossy | outrageous | pristine | raw |

a _____ buiding a _____ hotel room

_____ car a _____ piece of metal

a(n) _____ hairstyle a _____ exercise

GK + EK 12 Informal¹ – slang – very bad words

Match the words or word groups. Look at the example.

| ~~talkie~~ | bling bling | chill out | homie | be broke |
| ass | flossy | lettuce | dope | damn |

| a very bad word for a person that you hate | a very bad word that you use when you are angry | friend | glamorous | great |
| have no money | jewellery | money | relax | ~~sound film~~ |

talkie _____   sound film _____   _____   _____

_____   _____   _____   _____

_____   _____   _____   _____

_____   _____   _____   _____

_____   _____   _____   _____

¹informal [ɪnˈfɔːml] – *umgangssprachlich*

GK + EK 13 In a chat room

Answer sweetangel's message. Then write about your favourite song.
Write four sentences or more.

sweetangel, 21 June
Hi 2 all OneRepublic fans out there! At the moment I'm really crazy about their smash hit Apologize. It's a dope song n it sounds so damn good. Has any1 of U an idea what the rest of the album is like? …

Orange Line 4
ISBN 978-3-12-547544-1

© Ernst Klett Verlag GmbH, Stuttgart 2008 | www.klett.de
Von dieser Druckvorlage ist die Vervielfältigung für den eigenen Unterrichtsgebrauch gestattet. Die Kopiergebühren sind abgegolten. Alle Rechte vorbehalten.

Hi sweetangel,

EK **14 A song: Dear Mr President by Pink**

a) *Find the song text on the Internet and read it. Then read the message from an Internet forum below.*

Re: Dear Mr President 9 June

Hi yellow submarine,
As far as I know Pink once said in an interview that her song was an open letter to the President of the United States, George W. Bush, and that it was one of the most important songs she'd ever written. Pink also said that she wrote the song on Martin Luther King Day in 2005. She explained that she read *The New York Times* every day, and watched the news. She just needed to write that song. Hope I could help U. CU Rick

Released¹: 2006	Genre: Pop rock
Singer: Pink	Writer: Pink, Billymann
Album: I'm not dead	

¹to release [rɪˈliːs] – *veröffentlichen*

b) *Answer the questions.*

1. What does Pink suggest to Mr President?

2. What problems does Pink talk about in the third verse?

3. Why do you think the questions which Pink asks in the second verse and in the refrain are embarrassing for Mr President?

c) *Pink's song "Dear Mr President" got a lot of attention, not only in the US, but internationally, too. Read badboy's message. Why you think the song was discussed a lot?*

badboy, 21 June

Hi! Can any1 explain 2 me why some US radio stations don't play "Dear Mr President"?

Hi badboy, I don't know about any official reasons for that, but I think

 © Ernst Klett Verlag GmbH, Stuttgart 2008 | www.klett.de
Von dieser Druckvorlage ist die Vervielfältigung für den eigenen Unterrichtsgebrauch gestattet. Die Kopiergebühren sind abgegolten. Alle Rechte vorbehalten.

Orange Line 4
ISBN 978-3-12-547544-1

GK **15 Everyday English: In a music shop**

You are a customer in a music shop. You want to buy a CD. Complete the talk. Be polite.

Assistant: Can I help you?

You: _____

_____

Assistant: Do you know the name of the album?

You: _____

_____

Assistant: Let me see. I think I know which one you mean. Just a minute please. I'll get it for you. Here you are.

You: _____

_____

Assistant: We have special prices this week. So it's only $9.99.

You: _____

_____

Assistant: Thanks. Here you are. Have fun!

Tell the assistant what kind of music you want to buy. Tell him the name of the singer/band.

You are happy that they've got it and ask for the price.

You want to take it because it's cheap. Thank the assistant for his help and pay for the CD.

EK **15 Mixed bag: The Rolling Stones**

Complete the text with the missing words.

The Rolling Stones is an English rock band _____

was founded in 1962 _____ Brian Jones, Mick Jagger

und Keith Richards. In 1965 their song *I Can't Get No*

Satisfaction was their first number one hit in the US.

A few years later they were already one of the _____

famous rock bands _____ the world. They had a wild lifestyle, so they _____ soon

called the "bad boys" of the music scene. _____ more than 45 years in the music business the

band has made 55 albums and has had 32 UK and US top-10 singles. The Rolling Stones got a lot of

_____ for their music and performance, e.g. in 1989 the *Rock and Roll Hall of Fame* or in 2005

the *World Music Award* in the _____ *World's Greatest Touring Band of All Time*.

The photo was _____ in February 2008 when their _____ "Shine a light" was

_____. It shows *The Rolling Stones* on the _____ carpet of the 58th *Berlinale*.

Orange Line 4
ISBN 978-3-12-547544-1
© Ernst Klett Verlag GmbH, Stuttgart 2008 | www.klett.de
Von dieser Druckvorlage ist die Vervielfältigung für den eigenen Unterrichtsgebrauch
gestattet. Die Kopiergebühren sind abgegolten. Alle Rechte vorbehalten.

GK **16 Mediation and communication: A song: Dear Mr President**

Situation: Du bereitest eine Präsentation für den Musikunterricht vor. Dein Thema ist „Moderne Popsongs mit sozialkritischem Inhalt". Du möchtest u.a. auf „Dear Mr President" von Pink eingehen. Finde den Liedtext im Internet und lies ihn. Dann lies Ricks Nachricht.

Released[1]: 2006	Genre: Pop rock	Writer: Pink, Billymann
Singer: Pink	Album: I'm not dead	

Re: Dear Mr President 9 June

Hi there!
Well, as far as I know Pink once said in an interview that her song was an open letter to the President of the United States, George W. Bush, and that it was one of the most important songs she had ever written. Pink also said that she wrote the song on Martin Luther King Day in 2005. She explained that she read *The New York Times* every day, and watched the news. She just needed to write that song.
Hope I could help U.
CU Rick

1. Nenne wichtige Allgemeininformationen zum Lied.

2. Erkläre, wovon der Song handelt.

3. Gib einige Hintergrundinformationen zum Song.

4. Du hast gehört, dass manche US-Radiosender dieses Lied nicht spielen. Nenne einen möglichen Grund dafür.

[1]to release [rɪ'liːs] – *veröffentlichen*

© Ernst Klett Verlag GmbH, Stuttgart 2008 | www.klett.de
Von dieser Druckvorlage ist die Vervielfältigung für den eigenen Unterrichtsgebrauch gestattet. Die Kopiergebühren sind abgegolten. Alle Rechte vorbehalten.

Orange Line 4
ISBN 978-3-12-547544-1

EK **16 Mediation and communication: Goldene Kamera Awards**

Situation: Du bist mit einem Freund zur Verleihung der Goldenen Kamera.
Ihr hofft auf ein Interview mit einem internationalen Filmstar für eure Schülerzeitung.
Dein Freund ist für den Inhalt des Interviews zuständig. Deine Aufgabe ist, die Aussagen
aus dem bzw. ins Englische zu übertragen.

Pupils magaz!ne

** News, **
** infos **
** and
more **

Friend: Sie haben schon sehr viele Auszeichnungen bekommen.
Was bedeutet Ihnen die „Goldene Kamera"?

You: _____

Film star: It's a great thing to get this German television award and I'm really proud of it.

You: _____

_____

Friend: Wie viele Oscars haben Sie?

You: _____

Film star: I've got two Oscars.

You: _____

Friend: Wann haben Sie die Oscars erhalten?

You: _____

Film star: I was given my first Oscar in 1999 for "Girls never cry".
And I got another one in 2004 for "Thousand Dollar Kid".

You: _____

_____

_____

Friend: Sie haben auch einen Stern auf dem Hollywood Walk of Fame.
Wann haben Sie den bekommen?

You: _____

_____

Film star: In January 2007. My star is the 2,325th on Hollywood Boulevard, so you see that
I'm just one of the many really good stars.

You: _____

_____

Friend: Danke für das Interview. Viel Spaß hier in Berlin.

You: _____

_____

Orange Line 4
ISBN 978-3-12-547544-1

© Ernst Klett Verlag GmbH, Stuttgart 2008 | www.klett.de
Von dieser Druckvorlage ist die Vervielfältigung für den eigenen Unterrichtsgebrauch
gestattet. Die Kopiergebühren sind abgegolten. Alle Rechte vorbehalten.

Klett

Übersicht über die Aufgabentypen

		Aufgabe	Aufgabentyp	offen	halboffen	geschlossen	Schwerpunkte
1	GK	1a)–d)	Hörverstehen Detailverständnis			✔	Inhalt eines Gesprächs verstehen
	EK	1a), c), d)	Hörverstehen Detailverständnis			✔	Inhalt eines Gesprächs verstehen
	EK	1b)	Hörverstehen Globalverständnis			✔	
	GK+EK	2	Leseverstehen Detailverständnis			✔	Inhalt eines landeskundlichen Sachtextes lesend erfassen
	GK+EK	3	Grammatik			✔	Aussagen im *simple past*
	GK+EK	4	Grammatik			✔	Verneinung im *simple past*
	GK+EK	5a)	Grammatik			✔	Entscheidungsfragen im *simple past*
	GK+EK	5b)	Grammatik		✔		Fragen mit Fragewort im *simple past*
	GK	6	Grammatik			✔	Anwendung des *simple past*
	EK	6a)	Grammatik			✔	Aussagen im *past perfect*
	EK	6b)	Grammatik			✔	diskriminierende Anwendung von *simple past* und *past perfect*
	EK	7	Grammatik		✔		Verneinung im *past perfect*
	EK	8	Grammatik			✔	Fragen im *past perfect*
	GK	9	Schreiben/ Grammatik		✔		Anwendung des *simple past*
	EK	9	Schreiben	✔			Anwendung des *past perfect* in einer Mitteilung
	GK+EK	10	Lexik			✔	Bedeutung und Verwendung von Substantiven
	GK+EK	11	Lexik			✔	Anwendung von thematisch eingegrenztem Wortschatz
	EK	12	Lexik			✔	Unterscheidung von *BE* und *AE*
	GK+EK	13	Lexik			✔	Wortschatz „Geld in den USA"
	GK+EK	14	Lexik			✔	Erfassen von Paraphrasen und Zuordnung des entsprechenden Substantivs
	GK+EK	15	Lexik			✔	Wortschatz „Lebensmittel"
	GK+EK	16	Reagieren	✔			Reagieren in Alltagssituationen
	GK	17	Schreiben	✔			zusammenhängende Meinungsäußerung
	EK	17	Komplexübung			✔	Anwendung von sprachlichem Wissen
	GK+EK	18	Mediation			✔	wesentliche Informationen in der Muttersprache wiedergeben

		Aufgabe	Aufgabentyp	offen	halboffen	geschlossen	Schwerpunkte
2	GK+EK	1a)–c)	Hörverstehen Detailverständnis			✔	Inhalt eines Gesprächs über Freizeit hörend erfassen
	GK+EK	1d)	Hörverstehen Globalverständnis			✔	
	GK	2b)–d)	Leseverstehen Detailverständnis			✔	Informationen aus einem fiktiven Text lesend erfassen
	EK	2a)–d)	Leseverstehen Detailverständnis			✔	Informationen aus einem fiktiven Text lesend erfassen
	EK	3	Komplexübung			✔	Anwendung von sprachlichem Wissen
	GK+EK	4	Grammatik			✔	diskriminierende Anwendung von *have* oder *has* im *present perfect*

© Ernst Klett Verlag GmbH, Stuttgart 2008 | www.klett.de
Von dieser Druckvorlage ist die Vervielfältigung für den eigenen Unterrichtsgebrauch gestattet. Die Kopiergebühren sind abgegolten. Alle Rechte vorbehalten.

Orange Line 4
ISBN 978-3-12-547544-1

	Aufgabe	Aufgabentyp	offen	halboffen	geschlossen	Schwerpunkte
GK+EK	5a)	Grammatik			✔	Fragen im *present perfect*
GK+EK	5b)	Grammatik			✔	Verneinung im *present perfect*
GK+EK	6a)	Grammatik	✔			Fragen im *present perfect*
GK+EK	6b)	Grammatik	✔			positive und negative Aussagen im *present perfect*
GK	7	Schreiben	✔			Anwendung von *must, mustn't, needn't* und *can, can't* in einer vorgegebenen Situation
EK	7	Reagieren	✔			Anwendung von *should/shouldn't, may/may not, must/mustn't* in vorgegebenen Situationen
EK	8	Schreiben	✔			Anwendung von *should/shouldn't, may/may not, must/mustn't* in einer vorgegebenen Situation
GK+EK	9	Reagieren	✔			Anwendung sprachlichen Wissens und Könnens in vorgegebenen Situationen
GK+EK	10	Reagieren	✔			Anwendung sprachlichen Wissens und Könnens in einer vorgegebenen Situation
GK+EK	11	Schreiben	✔			Anwendung sprachlichen Wissens und Könnens in einer vorgegebenen Situation
GK+EK	12	Lexik			✔	Schulbegriffe *BE/AE*
GK+EK	13	Lexik			✔	Schultraditionen USA
GK+EK	14a)–b)	Lexik			✔	Bedeutung und Verwendung von Adjektiven
GK+EK	15	Lexik			✔	paraphrasierte Substantive
GK+EK	16	Lexik			✔	Bedeutung und Verwendung von Verben
GK+EK	17	Mediation			✔	wesentliche Informationen in der Muttersprache wiedergeben

		Aufgabe	Aufgabentyp	offen	halboffen	geschlossen	Schwerpunkte
3	GK	1a), b), d)	Hörverstehen Detailverständnis			✔	Inhalt eines Gespräches hörend erfassen
	GK	1c), e)	Hörverstehen Globalverständnis			✔	
	EK	1a)–d)	Hörverstehen Detailverständnis			✔	Inhalt eines Gespräches hörend erfassen
	EK	1e)	Hörverstehen Globalverständnis			✔	
	GK	2a)–c)	Leseverstehen Detailverständnis			✔	Informationen aus einem fiktiven Text lesend erfassen
	EK	2a)–d)	Leseverstehen Detailverständnis			✔	Informationen aus einem fiktiven Text lesend erfassen
	GK	3	Grammatik			✔	Steigerungsformen der Adjektive
	GK	4a)–d)	Grammatik	✔			Vergleichen: Gleichheit, Ungleichheit, Unterschiede und Superlative
	GK	5	Grammatik			✔	Anwendung der Steigerungsformen und des Vergleichens
	EK	3	Grammatik			✔	positive Aussagen im *passive simple present*
	EK	4a)	Grammatik			✔	Entscheidungsfragen im *passive simple present*
	EK	4b)	Grammatik		✔		positive und negative Aussagen im *passive simple present*

Orange Line 4
ISBN 978-3-12-547544-1

© Ernst Klett Verlag GmbH, Stuttgart 2008 | www.klett.de
Von dieser Druckvorlage ist die Vervielfältigung für den eigenen Unterrichtsgebrauch gestattet. Die Kopiergebühren sind abgegolten. Alle Rechte vorbehalten.

Klett

	Aufgabe	Aufgabentyp	offen	halboffen	geschlossen	Schwerpunkte
EK	5	Grammatik			✔	Fragen mit Fragewort im *passive simple present*
EK	6	Grammatik		✔		Aussagen im *passive simple present* zu einem vorgegebenen Thema
GK+EK	7	Lexik			✔	Lexik „Weltraum"
GK+EK	8	Lexik			✔	Lexik „Haushalt"
GK+EK	9a)	Lexik			✔	Bedeutung und Verwendung von Verben
GK+EK	9b)	Lexik		✔		
GK+EK	10	Lexik			✔	Antonyme
GK+EK	11	Lexik			✔	Wortfamilien
GK+EK	12	Lexik			✔	paraphrasierte Substantive
GK	13	Lexik			✔	paraphrasierte Begriffe
GK+EK	14	Reagieren	✔			Anwendung sprachlichen Wissens und Könnens in einer vorgegebenen Situation
GK	15	Schreiben	✔			Bedienung einer Mikrowelle
EK	15	Schreiben	✔			Erzählen einer fiktiven Geschichte
GK+EK	16	Reagieren	✔			Anwendung sprachlichen Wissens und Könnens in einer vorgegebenen Situation
EK	17	Komplexübung			✔	Anwendung von sprachlichem Wissen
GK	18	Mediation			✔	wesentliche Informationen in der Muttersprache wiedergeben
EK	18a)	Mediation		✔		Verständigen zu *false friends* in einer vorgegebenen Situation
EK	18b	Mediation		✔		wesentliche Informationen in der Fremdsprache wiedergeben

		Aufgabe	Aufgabentyp	offen	halboffen	geschlossen	Schwerpunkte
4	GK+EK	1a)-d)	Hörverstehen Detailverständnis			✔	Gespräch und Telefongespräch hörend erfassen
	GK+EK	1e)	Hörverstehen Globalverständnis			✔	
	EK	2	Schreiben		✔		Verfassen einer kurzen Benachrichtigung
	GK+EK	3	Reagieren	✔			Anwendung sprachlichen Wissens und Könnens in einer vorgegebenen Situation
	GK	4a)-d)	Leseverstehen Detailverständnis			✔	Informationen aus einem Sachtext lesend erfassen und verarbeiten
	EK	4a)-e)	Leseverstehen Detailverständnis			✔	Informationen aus einem Sachtext lesend erfassen und verarbeiten
	GK	5	Grammatik		✔		Anwendung der *conditional clauses Type I* - positive Aussagen
	GK	6	Grammatik		✔		Anwendung der *conditional clauses Type I* - Verneinung
	GK	7a)	Grammatik			✔	*conditional clauses Type I* - positive und negative Aussagen
	GK	7b)	Grammatik	✔			Anwendung der *conditional clauses Type I* - positive und negative Aussagen
	GK	8	Grammatik			✔	*conditional clauses Type I* - Fragen
	EK	5a)	Grammatik		✔		Anwendung der *conditional clauses Type I* - positive Aussagen

© Ernst Klett Verlag GmbH, Stuttgart 2008 | www.klett.de
Von dieser Druckvorlage ist die Vervielfältigung für den eigenen Unterrichtsgebrauch gestattet. Die Kopiergebühren sind abgegolten. Alle Rechte vorbehalten.

Orange Line 4
ISBN 978-3-12-547544-1

	Aufgabe	Aufgabentyp	offen	halboffen	geschlossen	Schwerpunkte
EK	5b)	Grammatik		✔		Anwendung der *conditional clauses* Type I – Verneinung
EK	6	Grammatik			✔	Anwendung der *conditional clauses* Type I – Aussagen und Fragen
EK	7a)	Grammatik			✔	*conditional clauses Type II* – positive und negative Aussagen
EK	7b)	Grammatik	✔			Anwendung der *conditional clauses* Type II – positive und negative Aussagen
EK	8	Grammatik			✔	*conditional clauses Type II* – Fragen
EK	9	Schreiben/ Grammatik	✔			Verfassen eines Sachtextes/ Anwendung der *conditional clauses* Type II
EK	10	Schreiben/ Grammatik	✔			Verfassen eines fiktiven Kurztextes/ Anwendung der *conditional clauses* Type II
GK+EK	11	Lexik			✔	Lexik zu einem vorgegebenen Sachverhalt
GK+EK	12	Lexik			✔	Anwendung von Lexik zu einem vorgegebenen Sachverhalt
GK+EK	13	Lexik			✔	Bedeutung und Verwendung von Verben
GK+EK	14	Lexik			✔	Bedeutung und Verwendung von Adjektiven
GK	15	Lexik			✔	Anwendung von Lexik zu einem vorgegebenen Thema
EK	15	Komplexübung			✔	Anwendung von sprachlichem Wissen
GK	16	Schreiben	✔			Verfassen eines Sachtextes
GK+EK	17	Mediation			✔	wesentliche Informationen in der Muttersprache wiedergeben

		Aufgabe	Aufgabentyp	offen	halboffen	geschlossen	Schwerpunkte
5	GK	1a)–b)	Hörverstehen Detailverständnis			✔	Informationen aus einem Gespräch hörend erfassen
	GK	1c)	Hörverstehen Globalverständnis			✔	
	EK	1a)–c)	Hörverstehen Detailverständnis			✔	Informationen aus einem Gespräch hörend erfassen
	EK	1d)	Hörverstehen Globalverständnis			✔	
	GK	2a)–b)	Leseverstehen Detailverständnis			✔	Informationen aus einem fiktiven Brief lesend erfassen
	EK	2a)–c)	Leseverstehen Detailverständnis			✔	Informationen aus einem fiktiven Brief lesend erfassen
	GK	3	Grammatik			✔	diskriminierende Verwendung von *who* und *which*
	GK	4	Grammatik			✔	diskriminierende Verwendung von *who* und *which*
	GK	5	Grammatik		✔		Anwendung von *who* und *which*
	EK	3	Grammatik			✔	*passive simple past* – positive Aussagen
	EK	4	Grammatik			✔	*passive simple past* – Fragen
	EK	5	Grammatik			✔	*passive simple past* – positive und negative Aussagen
	EK	6a)	Grammatik			✔	*passive simple past* – Fragen
	EK	6b)	Grammatik			✔	*passive simple past* – positive Aussagen

Orange Line 4
ISBN 978-3-12-547544-1

© Ernst Klett Verlag GmbH, Stuttgart 2008 | www.klett.de
Von dieser Druckvorlage ist die Vervielfältigung für den eigenen Unterrichtsgebrauch gestattet. Die Kopiergebühren sind abgegolten. Alle Rechte vorbehalten.

GK+EK	7	Lexik			✔	Anwendung von Lexik zu einem vorgegebenen Thema
GK+EK	8	Lexik			✔	Musikbegriffe
GK+EK	9	Lexik			✔	Wortfamilien
GK+EK	10	Lexik			✔	Bedeutung und Verwendung von Verben
GK+EK	11	Lexik			✔	Bedeutung und Verwendung von Adjektiven
GK+EK	12	Lexik			✔	Bedeutung und Verwendung von stilistisch gefärbter Lexik
GK+EK	13	Schreiben	✔			auf eine Frage aus einem Forum zusammenhängend antworten
EK	14	Lesen/Schreiben	✔			Liedtext und Text aus einem Forum lesend erfassen, deren Aussagen interpretieren und die eigene Meinung äußern
GK	15	Reagieren	✔			Anwendung sprachlichen Wissens und Könnens in einer vorgegebenen Situation
EK	15	Komplexübung			✔	Anwendung von sprachlichem Wissen
GK	16	Mediation			✔	wesentliche Informationen in der Muttersprache wiedergeben
EK	16	Mediation			✔	Mitteln/Reagieren in einer vorgegebenen Situation

© Ernst Klett Verlag GmbH, Stuttgart 2008 | www.klett.de
Von dieser Druckvorlage ist die Vervielfältigung für den eigenen Unterrichtsgebrauch gestattet. Die Kopiergebühren sind abgegolten. Alle Rechte vorbehalten.

Orange Line 4
ISBN 978-3-12-547544-1

Mündliche Lernerfolgskontrollen

1. Vorbemerkungen

Die Bildungsstandards der KMK für die erste Fremdsprache für den mittleren Schulabschluss verstehen unter kommunikativer Kompetenz im Sprechen

1. die Teilnahme an Gesprächen und
2. das zusammenhängende Sprechen.

Dies wird wie folgt präzisiert:

1. „Die Schülerinnen und Schüler können
   - an Gesprächen über vertraute Themen teilnehmen,
   - persönliche Meinungen ausdrücken und
   - Informationen austauschen. (B1)."

2. „Die Schülerinnen und Schüler können
   - Erfahrungen und Sachverhalte zusammenhängend darstellen,
     z.B. beschreiben, berichten, erzählen und bewerten (B1)."

Diese Ziele sind bis zum Ende der Sekundarstufe I verlässlich auszubilden, und zwar im Wesentlichen auf dem Niveau B1 des Gemeinsamen europäischen Referenzrahmens.

Mit Blick auf diese Niveaubeschreibung für den mittleren Schaulabschluss erscheint für die Klassenstufe 8 u. a. das Umsetzen nachfolgender Intentionen als zweckmäßig:

- Aufnehmen und Aufrechterhalten von sozialen Kontakten,
- Initiieren und Fortführen von sprachlichem Handeln,
- Äußern von/Reagieren auf Gefühle,
- Äußern von/Reagieren auf Meinungen und
- Einholen und Übermitteln von Informationen.

Diese Intentionen können z. B. in folgenden Sprechsituationen/Formen der mündlichen Leistung umgesetzt werden:

- Führen von Gesprächen zu Alltagssituationen,
- Führen von themengebundenen Gesprächen und
- zusammenhängendes Äußern in beschreibender, erzählender, berichtender und/oder wertender Form (auch als Teil eines Gesprächs).

Die nachfolgenden Vorschläge für mündliche Lernerfolgkontrollen orientieren sich an o. g. Intentionen und Sprechsituationen/Formen der mündlichen Leistung. Sie ermöglichen die Auswahl bestimmter Intentionen und Formen. Ziel sollte sein, Thema, Intention und Sprechsituation in bestmöglichen Einklang miteinander zu bringen. Selbstverständlich sind bei den einzelnen Themen auch andere Intentionen und Formen denkbar.

Der vorgeschlagene Inhalt der mündlichen Leistung bezieht sich immer auf das maximal Mögliche. Das notwendige Anpassen an die jeweilige Klassensituation kann relativ unkompliziert erfolgen, oft schon durch alleiniges Reduzieren.
In der Klassenstufe 8 stellt erfahrungsgemäß das sprachliche und inhaltliche Lenken der Schülerinnen und Schüler noch eine wichtige Voraussetzung für den Lernerfolg dar.
Aus diesem Grund wurde diesem didaktischen Prinzip große Aufmerksamkeit gewidmet.
Es werden detaillierte Vorschläge zur Lenkung angeboten, und zwar als sofort einsetzbare Kopiervorlagen. Ein großer Teil dieser Kopiervorlagen erfüllt parallel noch eine andere Funktion: sie können ebenso zur Erarbeitung des Stoffes im Vorfeld eingesetzt werden.

Orange Line 4
ISBN 978-3-12-547544-1

© Ernst Klett Verlag GmbH, Stuttgart 2008 | www.klett.de
Von dieser Druckvorlage ist die Vervielfältigung für den eigenen Unterrichtsgebrauch gestattet. Die Kopiergebühren sind abgegolten. Alle Rechte vorbehalten.

2. Bewertung

Die Beschreibung der mündlichen Sprachkompetenz für die Klassenstufe 8 kann folgendermaßen aussehen:

Die Äußerungen der Schülerinnen und Schüler erfolgen
- in stark variierten Situationen bzw. fortschreitend anwendungsbezogen,
- in fortschreitend anspruchsvolleren syntaktischen Strukturen,
- mit themen- und situationsbezogenem Wortschatz sowie fortschreitend mit eigenem Wortschatz,
- verständlich,
- überwiegend sprachlich korrekt,
- überwiegend adressaten- und situationsgerecht und
- überwiegend selbstständig.

Diesem Rechnung tragend, könnten zur Bewertung der mündlichen Leistung der Schülerinnen und Schüler in Klassenstufe 8 folgende Kriterien und Abstufungsgrade herangezogen werden:

Bewertung der Sprachkompetenz						
Kriterien/deren Erfüllung	voll	nahezu	im Wesentlichen	teilweise	kaum	nicht
inhaltlich richtig						
inhaltlich vollständig/ ausführlich						
sprachlich verständlich						
sprachlich korrekt						
phonetisch korrekt						
intonatorisch korrekt	*	*				
adressaten-/ situationsgerecht						
selbstständig						

*Diese Erfüllungsgrade stellen eine außerordentliche Leistung dar und können auch als solche gewertet werden.

3. Vorschläge für mündliche Lernerfolgskontrollen

Unit	Thema	Aufgabe	Form der mündlichen Leistung
1	Landeskunde USA	**GK + EK** *Talk about the Statue of Liberty. Use the facts from the fact box.*	zusammenhängendes Äußern zu einem vorgegebenen Thema/ Anwendung des *simple past*
	Alltagsleben/Freizeit	*At Diego's Deli* **GK** *Partner A: You are a waiter at Diego's Deli. You ask the guest what he/she would like. Make a dialogue with your partner. Be polite.* *Partner B: You and your friend are at Diego's Deli. You want to have breakfast. The waiter asks you what he/she can do for you. Make a dialogue with your partner. Be polite.*	sinngemäßes Übertragen in einer Alltagssituation

© Ernst Klett Verlag GmbH, Stuttgart 2008 | www.klett.de
Von dieser Druckvorlage ist die Vervielfältigung für den eigenen Unterrichtsgebrauch gestattet. Die Kopiergebühren sind abgegolten. Alle Rechte vorbehalten.

Orange Line 4
ISBN 978-3-12-547544-1

	Alltagsleben/Freizeit	**EK** *Partner A: You are a waiter at Diego's Deli. You ask the guest what he/she would like. Make a dialogue with your partner. Say it in English.* *Partner B: You and your friend are at Diego's Deli. You want to have breakfast. The waiter asks you what he/she can do for you. Make a dialogue with your partner. Say it in English.*	sinngemäßes Übertragen in einer Alltagssituation
	Freizeit/Interessen	*From bodybuilder to actor to Governor* **GK + EK** *Talk about Arnold Schwarzenegger's life.*	zusammenhängendes Äußern zu einem vorgegebenen Thema/ Anwendung des *simple past* und *past perfect*
2	Schule/Debattieren über ein kontroverses Thema	*Should we start the tradition of a school dance at our school?* **GK** *Your class wants to have a discussion on "Should we start the tradition of a school dance at our school?" One of you is the chairperson. Four other pupils are the speakers for and against school dances at your school. The others are the audience.* **EK** *Your class wants to have a debate on "Should we start the tradition of a school dance at our school?" One of you is the chairperson. Four other pupils are the speakers for and against the motion. The others are the audience.*	sprachliches Interagieren mit mehreren Partnern innerhalb eines themengebundenen Gesprächs
	Alltagsleben/Freizeit	*A talk with a good friend* **GK** *Partner A: You want to date someone and ask your friend for advice. Make a dialogue with your partner.* *Partner B: Your friend wants to date someone and asks you for advice.* *Make a dialogue with your partner.* **EK** *Partner A: You want to date someone and ask your friend for advice.* *Make a dialogue with your partner. Say it in English.* *Partner B: Your friend wants to date someone and asks you for advice.* *Make a dialogue with your partner. Say it in English.*	sinngemäßes Übertragen in einer Alltagssituation
	Alltagsleben/Freizeit	*Your friend's date wasn't a success.* **GK** *What do you say in these situations?* *Try to help him/her. Look at the clues.* **EK** *What do you say in these situations?* *Try to cheer him/her up. Look at the clues.*	isoliertes Äußern zu vorgegebenen Situationen
	Alltagsleben/ Empfehlungen geben	**GK** *Give eight good tips. Use 'can/can't', 'should', 'must/ mustn't', 'needn't'.*	isoliertes Äußern zu einer vorgegebenen Situation/ Anwendung modale Hilfsverben
3	Freizeit/Interessen	*A smart invention: a homework robot* **GK + EK** *Imagine you have bought a great invention: a homework robot. Tell your class about it.*	zusammenhängendes Äußern in wertender, beschreibender und darstellender Form

Orange Line 4
ISBN 978-3-12-547544-1

© Ernst Klett Verlag GmbH, Stuttgart 2008 | www.klett.de
Von dieser Druckvorlage ist die Vervielfältigung für den eigenen Unterrichtsgebrauch
gestattet. Die Kopiergebühren sind abgegolten. Alle Rechte vorbehalten.

	Alltagsleben/ Freizeit	*I'm afraid there's something wrong with …* **GK** *Partner A: You work at the reception of a motel. A guest phones you and asks you for help. Make a dialogue with your partner.* *Partner B: You are a guest at a motel. There's something wrong with some things in your room. You phone the reception desk. Make a dialogue with your partner.* **EK** *Partner A: You work at the reception of a motel. A guest phones you and asks you for help. Make a dialogue with your partner.* *Say it in English.* *Partner B: You are a guest at a motel. There's something wrong with some things in your room. You phone the reception desk. Make a dialogue with your partner. Say it in English.*	sinngemäßes Übertragen in einer Alltagssituation
	Alltagsleben/Vorgangs-beschreibung	*A useful invention: instant chocolate or coffee drinks* **GK + EK** *Explain how to use instant chocolate or coffee drinks. (Maybe you can bring different sorts of instant chocolate or coffee drinks to the lesson.)*	zusammenhängendes Äußern in beschreibender Form/Anwendung des *passive simple present*
	Freizeit/Interessen	*Phones and mobiles* **GK** *Compare the three phones.*	zusammenhängendes Äußern in vergleichender Form/Anwendung der Steigerung von Adjektiven
4	Alltagsleben/ Versprechen und Warnungen	*If …, I'll …* **GK** *What do you say in these situations.* *Use 'if'-clauses Type I.* *Promises and warnings* **EK** *What do you say in these situations?* *Use conditional clauses Type I to give a promise or a warning.*	isoliertes Äußern in vorgegebenen Situationen/ Anwendung des *conditional I*
	Freizeit/Tourismus	*Now that you've got the money …* **GK** *Imagine you're the star of a famous TV quiz show and you've just won the money for a big journey. Your partner is a reporter for a teenagers' magazine and wants to interview you.* *Make up the interview.*	sprachliches Interagieren mit einem Partner innerhalb eines themengebundenen Gesprächs
	Alltagsleben/ Vorgestelltes äußern	*If I …* **EK** *Choose four situations and say what you would do.*	isoliertes Äußern in vorgegebenen Situationen/ Anwendung des *conditional II*
	Freizeit/Tourismus	**GK** *Talk about two or three places in the US that you'd like to see. Bring some pictures to the lesson. Ask your teacher for a map of the US. Say eight sentences or more.*	zusammenhängendes Äußern zu einem vorgegebenen Thema
	Freizeit/Tourismus	**EK** *Imagine you're the star of a famous TV quiz show and you've just won a lot of money. Your partner is a reporter of a famous magazine and wants to interview you. Make up the interview.*	sprachliches Interagieren mit einem Partner innerhalb eines themengebundenen Gesprächs

 © Ernst Klett Verlag GmbH, Stuttgart 2008 | www.klett.de
Von dieser Druckvorlage ist die Vervielfältigung für den eigenen Unterrichtsgebrauch gestattet. Die Kopiergebühren sind abgegolten. Alle Rechte vorbehalten.

Orange Line 4
ISBN 978-3-12-547544-1

	Freizeit/Tourismus	**EK** *Talk about a journey (for example an adventure trip, a trip to the US or to Africa ...) which you would like to go on. Imagine that money was no problem.*	zusammenhängendes Äußern zu einem vorgegebenen Thema
5	Freizeit/Interessen	*A good song/One of my favourite songs* **GK + EK** *Present one of your favourite songs in class. Collect information and make notes. Bring a CD of the song, the lyrics and any pictures, posters, etc. to the lesson.*	zusammenhängendes Äußern in darstellender und wertender Form im Rahmen einer Präsentation
	Freizeit/Interessen	*Invitation to a film evening* **GK** (2 Varianten) *Partner A: You've got DVDs with Charlie Chaplin films. You want to invite your friend to a Chaplin evening. Make a dialogue with your partner.* *Partner B: Your friend invites you to a Charlie Chaplin film evening. You don't know any Chaplin films. Make a dialogue with your partner.* **EK** *Partner A: You've got DVDs with Charlie Chaplin films. You want to invite your friend to a Chaplin evening. Make a dialogue with your partner. Say it in English.* *Partner B: Your friend invites you to a Charlie Chaplin film evening. You don't know any Chaplin films. Make a dialogue with your partner. Say it in English.*	Variante 1: sinngemäßes Übertragen in einer Alltagssituation Variante 2: sprachliches Interagieren mit einem Partner innerhalb eines themengebundenen Gesprächs sinngemäßes Übertragen in einer Alltagssituation
	Geschichte/Interessen	**GK** *Talk about six of the following "Firsts".* **EK** *Talk about seven or eight "Firsts".*	isoliertes Äußern zu ausgewählten Sachverhalten/ Anwendung von Relativsätzen zusammenhängendes Äußern zu ausgewählten Sachverhalten/ Anwendung des *passive simple past*

Orange Line 4
ISBN 978-3-12-547544-1

© Ernst Klett Verlag GmbH, Stuttgart 2008 | www.klett.de
Von dieser Druckvorlage ist die Vervielfältigung für den eigenen Unterrichtsgebrauch gestattet. Die Kopiergebühren sind abgegolten. Alle Rechte vorbehalten.

4. Kopiervorlagen für die mündlichen Lernerfolgskontrollen

Unit 1

1. *Talk about the Statue of Liberty. Use the facts from the fact box.*
   Start your talk with an introduction and end it in a nice way.

GK

The Statue of Liberty

WHAT:	• a symbol of freedom • a sign of welcome to visitors and immigrants
WHERE:	• in New York Harbor • on Liberty Island
HISTORY:	• present from France to the US • Frederic Bartoldi/to make the plans in the 1870s • they/to begin to build the statue in France in 1882 • they/to finish it two years later • to bring it to the US by ship/in June 1885

EK

The Statue of Liberty

WHAT:	• a famous New York City landmark • a symbol of freedom • a sign of welcome to visitors • hope to millions of immigrants who/to arrive after 1886
WHERE:	• in New York Harbor • on Liberty Island
HISTORY:	• present from France to the US • Frederic Bartoldi/to design it in the 1870s • to begin to build the statue in 1882 • to finish it two years later • to bring it to the US by ship/in June 1885 • to put the statue into 350 pieces for the transport • workmen/to put the pieces together again • to open the statue to visitors/on October 28, 1886

 © Ernst Klett Verlag GmbH, Stuttgart 2008 | www.klett.de
Von dieser Druckvorlage ist die Vervielfältigung für den eigenen Unterrichtsgebrauch
gestattet. Die Kopiergebühren sind abgegolten. Alle Rechte vorbehalten.

Orange Line 4
ISBN 978-3-12-547544-1

2. At Diego's Deli
Use the menu in your book on page 12.

GK

Partner A: You are a waiter at Diego's Deli. You ask the guest what he/she would like. Make a dialogue with your partner. Be polite.	**Partner B:** You and your friend are at Diego's Deli. You want to have breakfast. The waiter asks you what he/she can do for you. Make a dialogue with your partner. Be polite.
You: Hello – help?	*(A: Hello, can I help you?)* You: Empire State Breakfast for two
(B: Hi, I'd like the Empire State Breakfast for two, please.) You: with or without coffee?	*(A: Would you like them with or without coffee?)* You: you – not want coffee
(B: Without coffee, please.) You: anything else to drink?	*(A: Would you like anything else to drink?)* You: yes – two milkshakes
(B: Yes, please. I'll take two milkshakes.) You: strawberry, cherry or banana?	*(A: Which ones would you like: strawberry, cherry or banana?)* You: you strawberry shake – your friend banana shake
(B: A strawberry shake for me and a banana shake for my friend, please.) You: Empire State Breakfast with bagels or toast?	*(A: Would you like bagels or toast with your Empire State Breakfast?)* You: bagels
(B: I'd like bagels, please.) You: anything else?	*(A: Anything else?)* You: no – thank waiter – that's all – ask for the price
(B: No, thanks. That's all. How much is it? You: $16.60	*(A: That's $16.60.)* You: give $17 – he/she can keep the change
(B: Here' $17. You can keep the change.) You: thank	*(A: Thanks.)*

EK

Partner A: You are a waiter at Diego's Deli. You ask the guest what he/she would like. Make a dialogue with your partner. Say it in English.	**Partner B:** You and your friend are at Diego's Deli. You want to have breakfast. The waiter asks you what he/she can do for you. Make a dialogue with your partner. Say it in English.
You: Hallo – dir helfen?	*(A: Hello, can I help you?)* You: Ja – zwei mal Empire State Breakfast.
(B: Hi, I'd like the Empire State Breakfast for two, please.) You: mit oder ohne Kaffee?	*(A: Would you like them with or without coffee?)* You: ohne Kaffee
(B: Without coffee, please.) You: etwas anderes zu trinken?	*(A: Would you like anything else to drink?)* You: zwei Milchshakes
(B: Yes, please. I'll take two milkshakes.) You: Erdbeere, Kirsche oder Banane?	*(A: Which ones would you like: strawberry, cherry or banana?)* You: Erdbeershake für mich – einen Bananenshake – Freund
(B: A strawberry shake for me and a banana shake for my friend, please.) You: Empire State Breakfast mit Bagels oder Toast?	*(A: Would you like bagels or toast with your Empire State Breakfast?)* You: Bagels
(B: I'd like bagels, please.) You: sonst noch etwas?	*(A: Anything else?)* You: Nein – danke – alles – kostet?
(B: No, thanks. That's all. How much is it?) You: $16.60	*(A: That's $16.60.)* You: $17 – Rest Trinkgeld
(B: Here's $17. You can keep the change.) You: Danke.	*(A: Thanks.)*

Orange Line 4
ISBN 978-3-12-547544-1

© Ernst Klett Verlag GmbH, Stuttgart 2008 | www.klett.de
Von dieser Druckvorlage ist die Vervielfältigung für den eigenen Unterrichtsgebrauch gestattet. Die Kopiergebühren sind abgegolten. Alle Rechte vorbehalten.

3. From bodybuilder to actor to Governor

GK *Talk about Arnold Schwarzenegger's life. Look at the clues. Use the simple past. Start your talk with an introduction and end it in a nice way.*

WHERE:		WHAT:
1. first/to live in Austria	⇨	there/to train[1] to be a bodybuilder
2. in 1966/to go to Germany	⇨	there/to win/the title "Mister Universe"/in 1967
3. in 1968/to immigrate to the US	⇨	in 1970/already to have some million dollars

in 1991/to start his fast food business "Planet Hollywood"

after that/to play in a lot of actions movies

in 1984/to get famous with his first "Terminator" movie

to work/as a actor/for about 20 years

then/to decide/to go into politics[2]

in 2003/to become 38th Governor[3] of the US State of California

[1]to train [treɪn] – *trainieren,* [2]politics ['pɒlɪtɪks] – *Politik,* [3]governor ['gʌvənə] – *Gouverneur*

EK *Talk about Arnold Schwarzenegger's life. Look at the clues. Use the simple past and the past perfect. Be careful. One sentence is in the simple present. Start your talk with an introduction and end it in a nice way.*

1. before/to immigrate to the US in 1968
   ⇨ to live in Austria and Germany

2. in Austria/to train to be a bodybuilder
   ⇨ before/to go to Germany/in 1966

3. in 1967/to win/the title 'Mister Universe' for the first time

4. in 1970/after two years in the US/already/ to become a millionaire

5. before/to start his fast food business 'Planet Hollywood'/in 1991 ⇨ to be/the owner of the famous restaurant 'Schatzi On Main' in Santa Monica

6. to play/in a lot of actions movies
   ⇨ before/to get famous with his first 'Terminator' movie/in 1984

7. after/to work/as a actor/for about 20 years
   ⇨ to decide/to go into politics[1]

8. in 2003/to become 38th Governor[2] of the US state of California

9. till today/to have the title 'Mr Olympia'
   ⇨ which/to win for the first time/in 1970

Example: 1. Before he immigrated to the US in 1968, he had lived in Austria and Germany.

[1]politics ['pɒlɪtɪks] – *Politik,* [2]governor ['gʌvənə] – *Gouverneur*

© Ernst Klett Verlag GmbH, Stuttgart 2008 | www.klett.de
Von dieser Druckvorlage ist die Vervielfältigung für den eigenen Unterrichtsgebrauch gestattet. Die Kopiergebühren sind abgegolten. Alle Rechte vorbehalten.

Orange Line 4
ISBN 978-3-12-547544-1

Unit 2

1. Should we start the tradition of a school dance at our school?

GK *Your class wants to have a discussion on "Should we start the tradition of a school dance at our school?" One of you is the chairperson. Four other pupils are the speakers for and against school dances at your school. The others are the audience.*
Use "Skills in action" in your book on page 34.

☞ Role A: You are the chairperson. Here is what you do and say:

> ➤ Welcome everybody to the discussion.
> ➤ Say that you are the chairperson today.
> ➤ Introduce the statement for today's discussion.
> ➤ Say something about the tradition of the Homecoming Dance in schools in the US.
> ➤ Introduce the speakers for and against school dances at your school.
> ➤ Ask the speakers for the school dance to start with their statement.
> ➤ *(Speakers for the school dance present their arguments.)*
> ➤ Thank them for their statement.
> ➤ Then ask the speakers against the school dance to present their arguments.
> ➤ *(Speakers against the school dance present their arguments.)*
> ➤ Thank them for their statement.
> ➤ Ask the audience who is for and who is against the school dance.
> ➤ Say who the winner is.

☞ Role B: You are a speaker **for** the school dance at your school. Prepare to say why it would be a good idea to start the tradition of a school dance at your school. Say three sentences or more.

> ♦ *For example:*
> - party
> - everyone should learn to dance
> - great event

☞ Role C: You are a speaker **against** the school dance at your school. Prepare to say why it would not be a good idea to start the tradition of a school dance at your school. Say three sentences or more.

> ♦ *For example:*
> - not everyone likes dancing
> - need expensive clothes
> - a lot of work to organize

EK *Your class wants to have a debate on "Should we start the tradition of a school dance at our school?" One of you is the chairperson. Four other pupils are the speakers for and against the motion. The others are the audience.*
Use "Skills in action" in your book on page 38.

☞ Role A: You are the chairperson. Here is what you do and say:

> ➤ Welcome everybody to the debate.
> ➤ Say that you are the chairperson of today's debate.
> ➤ Introduce the motion for today's debate.
> ➤ Say something about the tradition of the Homecoming Dance in schools in the US.
> ➤ Introduce the speakers for the motion and the speakers against the motion.
> ➤ Ask the speakers for the motion to start with their statement.
> ➤ *(Speakers for the motion present their arguments.)*
> ➤ Thank them for their statement.
> ➤ Then ask the speakers against the motion to present their arguments.
> ➤ *(Speakers against the motion present their arguments.)*
> ➤ Thank them for their statement.
> ➤ Ask the audience to vote for or against the motion.
> ➤ Present the results of the vote.

☞ Role B: You are a speaker **for** the motion. Prepare to argue why it would be a good idea to start the tradition of a school dance at your school. Say three sentences or more.

☞ Role C: You are a speaker **against** the motion. Prepare to argue why it would not be a good idea to start the tradition of a school dance at your school. Say three sentences or more.

Orange Line 4
ISBN 978-3-12-547544-1

© Ernst Klett Verlag GmbH, Stuttgart 2008 | www.klett.de
Von dieser Druckvorlage ist die Vervielfältigung für den eigenen Unterrichtsgebrauch gestattet. Die Kopiergebühren sind abgegolten. Alle Rechte vorbehalten.

2. A talk with a good friend

GK

Partner A: You want to date someone and ask your friend for advice. Make a dialogue with your partner.	Partner B: Your friend wants to date someone and asks you for advice. Make a dialogue with your partner.
You: Hi – I want to date *** – what say to ***?	(A: Hi, … I'd like to date *** What can I say to her/him?) You: think – you should be direct
(B: Well, I think you should be direct.) You: what we can do together?	(A: What can we do together?) You: *** likes to go to the movies?
(B: Does *** like to go to the movies?) You: yes – *** crazy about action movies	(A: Yes, *** does. *** is crazy about action movies.) You: action movie on at the moment?
(B: Is there an action movie on at the moment?) You: yes – [name of film] – what wear?	(A: Yes, there is. " …" is on. What should I wear?) You: can wear – not be late
(B: You can wear … And don't be late.) You: thank for tips – what say to *** when you meet?	(A: Thanks for your tips. What can I say when we meet?) You: something nice about hair or …
(B: Say something nice about *** hair, … or … , for example.) You: good idea – how end date if not so hot?	(A: That's a good idea. How can I end the date if it isn't so hot?) You: be polite and friendly when goodbye
(B: Be polite and friendly when you say goodbye.)	

*** name of the boy or girl you want to date *or* 'him'/'her' *or* 'his'/'her'

EK

Partner A: You want to date someone and ask your friend for advice. Make a dialogue with your partner. Say it in English.	Partner B: Your friend wants to date someone and asks you for advice. Make a dialogue with your partner. Say it in English.
You: würde gern verabreden mit … – aber weiß nicht, wie sie/ihn fragen	(A: Hi, … I'd like to date … but I don't know how I should ask her/him.) You: denke – direkt sein
(B: Well, I think you should be direct.) You: was ihr/ihm sagen? – Kino oder Pizza essen oder Eis essen?	(A: What should I tell her/him? Should I tell her/him that we could go to the movies or to Tonio's Pizza shop or have an ice-cream?) You: etwas zusammen tun, was beide mögen – nicht etwas vorschlagen, das nur dich interessiert
(B: You must do something together which you both like. You mustn't suggest anything that only you are interested in.) You: was anziehen?	(A: And what should I wear?) You: nicht komische Klamotten – sonst sie/er glaubt, dass Freak
(B: You mustn't wear strange clothes. She/ He may think you're a freak.) You: kleines Geschenk geben? – aber sie/er mag es vielleicht nicht	(A: Should I give her/him a little present? She/he may not like it.) You: gute Idee – aber nicht übertreiben – sie/er sonst vielleicht verlegen

 © Ernst Klett Verlag GmbH, Stuttgart 2008 | www.klett.de
 Von dieser Druckvorlage ist die Vervielfältigung für den eigenen Unterrichtsgebrauch gestattet. Die Kopiergebühren sind abgegolten. Alle Rechte vorbehalten.

Orange Line 4
 ISBN 978-3-12-547544-1

(B: That's a good idea. But you mustn't overdo it. She/He may feel embarrassed.) You: du hast Recht – weiß, was ihr/ihm schenken	(A: You're right. I think I know what I can give her/him.) You: weiß deine Schwester – du mit … verabredet?
(B: Does your sister know that you want to date …) You: nein! – ihr nicht sagen – Sie erzählt vielleicht Mutti – dann Fragen beantworten	(A: No, she doesn't. You mustn't tell her about it. She may tell Mum and then I'll have to answer all her questions.) You: OK – keine Sorge
(B: OK. Don't worry!)	

3. *Your friend's date wasn't a success.*
GK *What do you say in these situations? Try to help him/her.*
Look at the clues.

Let's …   How mean/awful/embarrassing …
Don't worry …   I'm sure he/she …
He's/She's wrong about …   I'm sorry …

EK *What do you say in these situations? Try to cheer him/her up.*
Look at the clues.

Cheer up …   How embarrassing …
Don't worry …
You're kidding …   I'm sorry …

Your friend tells you that …
1. his/her date wasn't so hot and he/she is unhappy.
2. his/her date laughed at the present.
3. his/her date said something hurtful about his/her hairstyle.
4. his/her date had told everyone that they were going out together.
5. everyone in class will laugh at him/her now.

GK 4. *Give eight good tips. Use 'can/can't', 'should', 'must/mustn't', 'needn't'.*

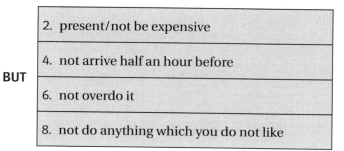

1. give your date a little present		2. present/not be expensive
3. not be late	**BUT**	4. not arrive half an hour before
5. say something nice when you meet		6. not overdo it
7. do something which your date likes		8. not do anything which you do not like

Orange Line 4
ISBN 978-3-12-547544-1

© Ernst Klett Verlag GmbH, Stuttgart 2008 | www.klett.de
Von dieser Druckvorlage ist die Vervielfältigung für den eigenen Unterrichtsgebrauch gestattet. Die Kopiergebühren sind abgegolten. Alle Rechte vorbehalten.

Klett

Unit 3

K + EK 1. A smart invention: a homework robot
Imagine you have bought a great invention: a homework robot. Tell your class about it.

- Start your talk with an introduction.
- Tell your class
  how smart/intelligent/useful/easy to operate ... your homework robot is.
- Describe
  - how you got it;
  - what your homework robot looks like. Name important parts
    and any extra equipment.
- Explain
  - what your homework robot can do, for example
    - what sort of homework it can do
    - what languages it speaks
    - what it can read or understand
    - ...
  - how you operate the robot, for example
    - by remote control, with a touch screen monitor ...
    - with a scanner, microphone ... .
- End your talk in a nice way.

2. I'm afraid there's something wrong with ...

GK

Partner A: You work at the reception of a motel. A guest phones you and asks you for help. Make a dialogue with your partner.	Partner B: You are a guest at a motel. There's something wrong with some things in your room. You phone the reception desk. Make a dialogue with your partner.
You: reception – ... speaking – how help?	*(A: Reception. Mr/Mrs ... speaking. How can I help you?)* You: something wrong with TV
(B: I'm afraid there's something wrong with the TV.) You: sorry – can switch the TV on and off?	*(A: I'm sorry to hear that. Can you switch the TV on and off?)* You: yes – but can't change channels – perhaps battery of remote control dead?
(B: Yes, I can. But I can't change channels. Maybe the battery of the remote control is dead.) You: will send someone up to fix – room number?	*(A: I'll send someone up to fix it. What's your room number, please?)* You: room number – another problem: can't switch on hair dryer
(B: Room ... I'm afraid I've got another problem. I can't switch on the hair dryer.) You: switched on little switch next to socket? – for electricity	*(A: Have you switched on the little switch next to the socket? It's for electricity.)* You: no – thank for tip
(B: No, I haven't. Thanks for the tip.) You: welcome – do anything else?	*(A: You're welcome. Can I do anything else for you?)* You: toothache – dentist near motel?
(B: I've got a toothache. Is there a dentist near here?) You: yes – bad pain – phone Dr Smith for you?	*(A: Yes, there is. Is the pain bad? I could phone Dr Smith for you.)* You: would be nice
(B: That would be nice.)	

 © Ernst Klett Verlag GmbH, Stuttgart 2008 | www.klett.de
Von dieser Druckvorlage ist die Vervielfältigung für den eigenen Unterrichtsgebrauch
gestattet. Die Kopiergebühren sind abgegolten. Alle Rechte vorbehalten.

Orange Line 4
ISBN 978-3-12-547544-1

EK

Partner A: You work at the reception of a motel. A guest phones you and asks you for help. Make a dialogue with your partner. Say it in English.	Partner B: You are a guest at a motel. There's something wrong with some things in your room. You phone the reception desk. Make a dialogue with your partner. Say it in English.
	(A: Reception. Mr/Mrs … speaking. What can I do for you?)
You: Rezeption – Herr/Frau … am Apparat – helfen?	You: etwas nicht in Ordnung mit Fernseher
(B: I'm afraid there's something wrong with the TV.)	(A: I'm sorry to hear that. Can you switch the TV on and off?)
You: tut mir leid – Gerät ein – und ausschalten?	You: ja – aber keine anderen Kanäle wählen – vielleicht Batterie der Fernbedienung tot?
(B: Yes, I can. But I can't choose any other channels. Maybe the battery of the remote control is dead.)	(A: I'll send someone up to fix it. What's your room number, please?)
You: schicke jemanden zum Reparieren – Zimmernummer?	You: 147 – anderes Problem – kann Fön nicht einschalten
(B: Room 147. I'm afraid I've got another problem. I can't switch on the hairdryer.)	(A: Have you switched on the little switch next to the socket? It's for electricity.)
You: kleinen Schalter neben Steckdose angeschaltet? – für Strom	You: nein – danke für Tipp
(B: No. I haven't. Thanks for the tip.)	(A: You're welcome. Can I do anything else for you?)
You: gern geschehen – noch etwas für Sie tun?	You: Zahnschmerzen – Zahnarzt in der Nähe?
(B: I've got a toothache. Is there a dentist near here?)	(A: Yes, there is. Is the pain bad? Should I phone Dr Smith for you?)
You: Ja – schlimme Schmerzen? – Dr. Smith anrufen?	You: sehr nett
(B: That would be nice.)	

GK + EK 3. A useful invention: instant[1] chocolate or coffee drinks

Explain how to use instant chocolate or coffee drinks. (Maybe you can bring different sorts of instant chocolate or coffee drinks to the lesson.) Look at the clues.

- Start your talk with an introduction.
- First say why instant chocolate or coffee drinks are a useful invention.
- Compare them with normal coffee and cocoa[2]. (good/tasty/easy to make/expensive …)
- Then name some popular sorts.
- Next explain how a chocolate or coffee drink is made. (Use: First …/Next …/Then …/Finally …)
- End your talk in a nice way.

1.	2.	3.	4.	5.
to fill	to heat[3]	to put	to add	to stir[4] well

[1]instant ['ɪnstənt] – *löslich*, [2]cocoa ['kəʊkəʊ] – *Kakao*, [3]to heat [hiːt] – *erhitzen*, [4]to stir [stɜː] – *umrühren*

Orange Line 4
ISBN 978-3-12-547544-1

© Ernst Klett Verlag GmbH, Stuttgart 2008 | www.klett.de
Von dieser Druckvorlage ist die Vervielfältigung für den eigenen Unterrichtsgebrauch gestattet. Die Kopiergebühren sind abgegolten. Alle Rechte vorbehalten.

GK 4. Phones and mobiles

Compare the three phones. Start your talk with an introduction and end it in a nice way.

call someone	✓	✓	✓
leave a message	✗	✓	✓
send a fax	✗	✓	✗
send a text	✗	✗	✓
play games	✗	✗	✓
surf the Internet	✗	✗	✓
take photos	✗	✗	✓
…			

Say which is …
- as good as/better than/the best of all because …
- as useful as/more useful than/the most useful of all because …
- as cheap as/cheaper than/the cheapest of all because …
- as expensive as/more expensive than/the most expensive of all when you think of the prices for a call, a message etc.
- as helpful as/more helpful than/the most helpful of all when you need to contact someone
- …

Unit 4

GK 1. If …, I'll …

What do you say in these situations. Use 'if'-clauses Type I. Look at the clues and the example.

do the shopping   feel sick   not help you with your homework any more

not give you my make-up any more   help with the work in the garden   hurt your fingers

1. You want to go to the movies.	⇨	Tell your mum what you'll do if she lets you go there.
2. You're crazy about some new jeans.	⇨	Tell your grandma what you'll do if she buys them.
3. The batteries of your MP3 player are dead.	⇨	Tell your brother what you'll do if he uses it again.
4. Your parents know about your new friend.	⇨	Tell your sister what you'll do if she tells your parents about a secret again.
5. Your little brother is playing with a knife.	⇨	Tell your bother what will happen if he isn't careful with the knife.
6. Your little sister has eaten a lot of sweets.	⇨	Tell your little sister what will happen if she doesn't stop eating sweets.

Example: 1. If you let me go to the movies, I'll do the shopping.

 © Ernst Klett Verlag GmbH, Stuttgart 2008 | www.klett.de
Von dieser Druckvorlage ist die Vervielfältigung für den eigenen Unterrichtsgebrauch gestattet. Die Kopiergebühren sind abgegolten. Alle Rechte vorbehalten.

Orange Line 4
ISBN 978-3-12-547544-1

EK 1. Promises and warnings

What do you say in these situations? Use conditional clauses Type I to give a promise or a warning.

1. You want to go to the movies. ⇨ Tell your mum what you promise you'll do if she lets you go there.

2. You are crazy about some new jeans. ⇨ Tell your grandma what you promise you'll do if she buys them.

3. The batteries of your MP3 player are dead. ⇨ Warn your brother about what you'll do if he uses it again.

4. Your parents know about your new friend. ⇨ Warn your sister about what you'll do if she tells your parents about a secret again.

5. Your little brother is playing with a knife. ⇨ Warn your little brother about what will happen if he isn't careful.

6. Your little sister has eaten a lot of sweets. ⇨ Warn your little sister about what will happen if she doesn't stop eating sweets.

GK 2. Now that you've got the money …

Imagine you're the star of a famous TV quiz show and you've just won the money for a big journey. Your partner is a reporter for a teenagers' magazine and wants to interview you. Make up the interview.

Reporter:	You:
1. Say hello and introduce yourself (name/name of the magazine you work for).	Say hello.
2. Ask him/her for an interview.	Say yes.
3. Say something nice about him/her and the TV quiz show.	Thank the reporter.
4. Say that you have heard that he/she will go on a journey to the US in the summer holidays.	Say that that is right.
5. Say that the readers of your magazine are interested in his/her travelling ideas. Then ask what parts of the US he/she wants to visit.	Tell the reporter what parts of the US you want to visit and why.
6. Ask who he/she wants take with him/her.	Tell the reporter who you want take with you and why.
7. Ask how he/she will travel to and around the US.	Tell the reporter about your ideas.
8. Ask him/her if you could take some photos.	Say yes.
9. Thank him/her for the interview. Wish him/her something nice.	Thank the reporter and say goodbye.

Orange Line 4
ISBN 978-3-12-547544-1
© Ernst Klett Verlag GmbH, Stuttgart 2008 | www.klett.de
Von dieser Druckvorlage ist die Vervielfältigung für den eigenen Unterrichtsgebrauch gestattet. Die Kopiergebühren sind abgegolten. Alle Rechte vorbehalten.

EK 2. *Choose four situations and say what you would do.*

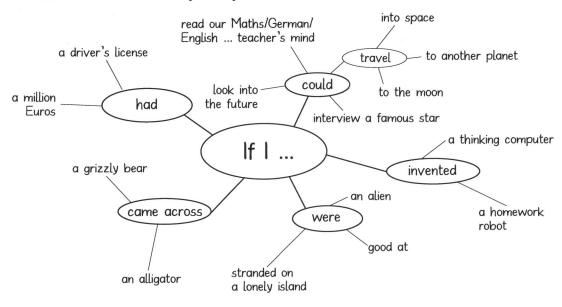

GK 3. *Talk about two or three places in the US that you'd like to see. Bring some pictures to the lesson. Ask your teacher for a map of the US. Say eight sentences or more. Start your talk with an introduction and end it in a nice way.*

Say ...
- where the places are in the US
  (for example: in the state of ..., on the east/west coast, in the north/south/... of ...,
  in the ... Mountains; near Lake ...) and show them on the map
- why they're so interesting for you
- what you can see and do there

EK 3. *Imagine you're the star of a famous TV quiz show and you've just won a lot of money. Your partner is a reporter of a famous magazine and wants to interview you. Make up the interview.*

Reporter:	You:
1. Say hello and introduce yourself (name/name of the magazine you work for).	Say hello.
2. Ask him/her for an interview.	Agree.
3. Say something nice about his/her success in the TV quiz show.	Thank the reporter.
4. Say that you have heard that he/she would like to go on a big journey.	Say that that is right.
5. Say that the readers of your magazine are interested in his/her travelling ideas. Then ask where he/she would like to go.	Tell the reporter where you would like to go and why.
6. Ask who he/she would take with him/her.	Tell the reporter who you would take with you and why.
7. Ask what he/she would like to see and do on the journey.	Tell the reporter about your ideas.
8. Ask him/her if you could take some photos.	Agree.
9. Thank him/her for the interview. Wish him/her something nice.	Thank the reporter and say goodbye.

 © Ernst Klett Verlag GmbH, Stuttgart 2008 | www.klett.de
Von dieser Druckvorlage ist die Vervielfältigung für den eigenen Unterrichtsgebrauch gestattet. Die Kopiergebühren sind abgegolten. Alle Rechte vorbehalten.

Orange Line 4
ISBN 978-3-12-547544-1

EK 4. *Talk about a journey (for example an adventure trip, a trip to the US or to Africa ...) which you would like to go on. Imagine that money was no problem. Start your talk with an introduction and end it in a nice way.*

Say
• where you'd like to go. Why?
• who you'd take with you. Why?
• how you'd travel.
• what you'd need for your trip.
• what you'd like to see and do.
• where you'd stay/spend the nights.
• ...

Unit 5

1. *Present one of your favourite songs in class. Collect information and make notes. Bring a CD of the song, the lyrics and any pictures, posters, etc. to the lesson.*
   The mind map below gives you an idea of how you should collect your info and how you can structure (gliedern) your talk. Start your talk with an introduction and end it in a nice way.

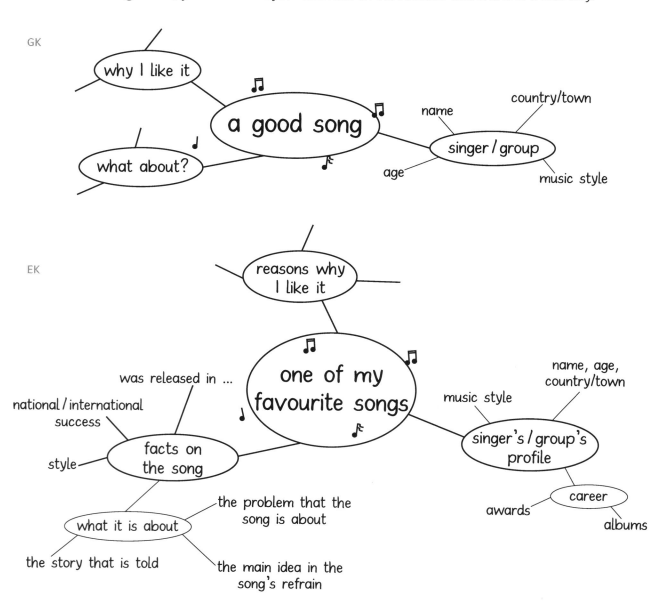

Orange Line 4
ISBN 978-3-12-547544-1

© Ernst Klett Verlag GmbH, Stuttgart 2008 | www.klett.de
Von dieser Druckvorlage ist die Vervielfältigung für den eigenen Unterrichtsgebrauch gestattet. Die Kopiergebühren sind abgegolten. Alle Rechte vorbehalten.

2. Invitation to a film evening

GK **Variante 1**

Partner A: You've got DVDs with Charlie Chaplin films. You want to invite your friend to a Chaplin evening. Make a dialogue with your partner.	Partner B: Your friend invites you to a Charlie Chaplin film evening. You don't know any Chaplin films. Make a dialogue with your partner.
You: interested in old Charlie Chaplin films? – watch some at your place tonight	(A: Are you interested in the old Charlie Chaplin films? We could watch some at my place tonight.) You: interested – never seen a Charlie Chaplin film – how old those films?
(B: Why not? I've never seen any Chaplin films before. How old are they?) You: about 70 years old – know that they are silent pictures?	(A: About a hundred years. Do you know that they are silent pictures?) You: silent pictures? – never heard – what?
(B: Silent pictures? I've never heard of them. What are silent pictures?) You: without sound	(A: The first movies which they made didn't have sound.) You: can't believe – how understand what film was about?
(B: No sound? I can't believe that. How could you understand what the film was about?) You: sometimes words on the screen – or actors had to be good	(A: Sometimes they showed the words on the screen. The actors had to be good because you couldn't hear what they said.) You: not sure if like silent pictures – Charlie Chaplin was good actor?
(B: Well, I'm not so sure if I like silent pictures. Was Charlie Chaplin a good actor?) You: yes – if don't like silent pictures, watch …?	(A: Yes, he was. But if you don't like silent pictures, we can watch …) You: OK – bring other DVDs like …
(B: OK./Good idea. I can bring …)	

Variante 2

Partner A: You've got DVDs with Charlie Chaplin films. You want to invite your friend to a Chaplin evening. Make a dialogue with your partner.	Partner B: Your friend invites you to a Charlie Chaplin film evening. You don't know any Chaplin films. Make a dialogue with your partner.
1. Invite your friend to a Charlie Chaplin evening.	2. You're interested in it because you have never seen a Charlie Chaplin film before.
3. Explain that they're silent pictures and that they're very old.	4. You don't know what silent pictures are. You want to know more about such films.
5. Explain what silent pictures are.	6. You're surprised. You're not so sure if it's a good idea to watch such movies all evening.
7. Make a suggestion of what you can do if your partner doesn't like them.	8. Make another suggestion and ask your partner for his/her opinion.

 © Ernst Klett Verlag GmbH, Stuttgart 2008 | www.klett.de
Von dieser Druckvorlage ist die Vervielfältigung für den eigenen Unterrichtsgebrauch gestattet. Die Kopiergebühren sind abgegolten. Alle Rechte vorbehalten.

Orange Line 4
ISBN 978-3-12-547544-1

EK

Partner A: You've got DVDs with Charlie Chaplin films. You want to invite your friend to a Chaplin evening. Make a dialogue with your partner. Say it in English.	**Partner B:** Your friend invites you to a Charlie Chaplin film evening. You don't know any Chaplin films. Make a dialogue with your partner. Say it in English.
You: an den alten Charlie-Chaplin-Filmen interessiert? – könnten heute Abend einige anschauen bei mir	(A: Are you interested in the old Charlie Chaplin films? We could watch some at my place tonight.) You: warum nicht? – noch nie Chaplin-Filme gesehen – wann produziert?
(B: Why not? I've never seen any Chaplin films before. When were they made?) You: vor ca. 70 Jahren – Stummfilme	(A: About a hundred years ago. Do you know that they are still pictures?) You: Stummfilme? – noch nie gehört – was sind Stummfilme?
(B: Still pictures? I've never heard of them. What are still pictures?) You: Filme, die keinen Ton haben	(A: The first movies which were produced didn't have a sound.) You: aber wie verstehen, wovon der Film handelte?
(B: No sound? But how could you understand what the film was about?) You: manchmal Texte auf Leinwand – wenn Schauspieler gut, konnte man erraten, was sie sagten	(A: Sometimes the words were shown on the screen. If the actors were good, you could guess what they wanted to say.) You: wie lange Stummfilme gemacht?
(B: How long were still pictures produced?) You: bis ca. 1930 – erster Tonfilm 1927	(A: Until about 1930. I think the first talkie was shown in 1927.) You: den Schauspielern damals schon Auszeichnungen verliehen?
(B: Were the actors given awards at that time?) You: glaube, Oscars sehr alt	(A: I believe the Oscars are very old awards.) You: Emil Jannings erster deutscher Schauspieler, der Oscar bekam
(B: I only know that Emil Jannings was the first German actor who was given an Oscar.)	

Orange Line 4
ISBN 978-3-12-547544-1

© Ernst Klett Verlag GmbH, Stuttgart 2008 | www.klett.de
Von dieser Druckvorlage ist die Vervielfältigung für den eigenen Unterrichtsgebrauch gestattet. Die Kopiergebühren sind abgegolten. Alle Rechte vorbehalten.

GK 3. *Ta!k about <u>six</u> of the following "Firsts". Start your talk with an introduction and end it in a nice way. You can begin like this:*

I'd like to talk about some famous inventions and important events of the past.
Let me begin with the telephone. It's a very old invention. The first sentence which a man spoke over the telephone was "A horse doesn't eat cucumber salad." That was in 1861.
Now I'll tell you something about …

1861

"A horse doesn't eat cucumber salad."

- The first sentence who/which a man/to speak over the telephone was …
- That/to be in …

cucumber ['kjuːkʌmbə] – *Gurke*

1873

- Gold diggers/to be the first people who/which to wear/Levis jeans.
- That/to be in …

digger ['dɪgə] – *der Gräber*

1876

- The ketchup, who/which people/to eat in 1876, was not tomato ketchup

1879

- T. A. Edison who/which to be/famous inventor, also invented …

1886

- Coke, who/which to be not/a hit from the start, became popular after 1890
- Dr Pemberton, who/which to invent/this drink in 1886, first sold about nine glasses every day

1952

- In 1952 there/to be/about 300 people in Germany who/which to watch/the first regular programmes on German TV

July 20, 1969

- The first men who/which set foot on the moon/ to be Neil Armstrong and Buzz Aldrin.
- On their "moon walk", who/which to last/ 2.5 hours, they planted the flag …
- That/to be on …

to set [set] – *setzen*,
to plant [plɑːnt] – *hier: aufstellen*

© Ernst Klett Verlag GmbH, Stuttgart 2008 | www.klett.de
Von dieser Druckvorlage ist die Vervielfältigung für den eigenen Unterrichtsgebrauch gestattet. Die Kopiergebühren sind abgegolten. Alle Rechte vorbehalten.

Orange Line 4
ISBN 978-3-12-547544-1

EK 3. *Talk about seven or eight "Firsts". Start your talk with an introduction and end it in a nice way. You may begin like this:*

I'd like to talk about some famous inventions and important events of the past.
Let me begin with the telephone. It is a very old invention. …

1861  "A horse doesn't eat cucumber salad." • The first sentence/which/to speak over the telephone in … <div align="right">cucumber ['kjuːkʌmbə] – *Gurke*</div>	**1873**  • first/to wear/in …/by gold diggers <div align="right">digger ['dɪgə] – *der Gräber*</div>
1876  • to eat/for the first time/in … • to not make/from tomatoes at that time	**1879** • to invent/in …/by Thomas A. Edison
1886  • to produce/for the first time/in … • first/only about nine glasses a day/to sell	**1990**  • in … clothes/to wash/in an electric washing machine/for the first time • but at that time/the motor/to not protect from dripping water – dangerous!
1927  • in …/the first non-stop flight across the Atlantic/to make/by Charles Lindbergh	**1952**  • first regular programmes in German TV/to show/in … • the programmes/to watch/by about 300 people
July 20, 1969  • first steps on the moon/to make/ by Neil Armstrong/in …	**August 5, 1991** • in 1989/the idea of the hypertext/to develop by Tim Berners-Lee • the World Wide Web/to be born • the first web site/to put online on …

Orange Line 4
ISBN 978-3-12-547544-1

© Ernst Klett Verlag GmbH, Stuttgart 2008 | www.klett.de
Von dieser Druckvorlage ist die Vervielfältigung für den eigenen Unterrichtsgebrauch gestattet. Die Kopiergebühren sind abgegolten. Alle Rechte vorbehalten.

Klett

Illustrationen:
Simone Pahl, Berlin
(alle außer S.9: (1) Dorothee Wolters, Köln; S.13: (1-2) Klett-Archiv, Stuttgart; S.25: (1-2) Sven Palmowski, Barcelona; (3-4) David Norman, Meerbusch; (5) Boris Goldammer, Berlin; (6) Ulrike Eisenbraun, Bad Urach; (7) Carolin Ina Schröter, Berlin; (8) Dorothee Wolters, Köln; S. 27: (1) Sylvia Wolff, Wiesbaden; S.39: (1-2) Gerlinde Keller, München; S.45: (1) Karin Mall, Berlin; (2) Helga Merkle, Albershausen; S.53: (1) Marlene Pohle, Stuttgart; S.56: (1) Michael Luz, Stuttgart; (2) Pawel Miedzinski, Kozieglowy; (3) Volkmar Döring, Bingen a. R.; (4) Klett-Archiv, Stuttgart; S.68: (1, 8, 11) Klett-Archiv, Stuttgart; (2, 9, 10) Athos Boncompagni, Arezzo; (3, 7, 13) Klett-Archiv, Stuttgart; (4, 6, 14) David Norman, Meerbusch; (5, 12) Christian Dekelver, Weinstadt; S.94: (1) David Norman, Meerbusch; S.101: (1) Tom Menzel, Rohlsdorf; S.102: (1) Tom Menzel, Rohlsdorf)

Bildquellenverzeichnis:
S.5: (1) laif (Keystone France), Köln; S.15: (1-4) Klett-Archiv, Stuttgart; S.16: (1) iStockphoto (SharonDay), Calgary, Alberta; (2) iStockphoto (matka_Wariatka), Calgary, Alberta; (3) iStockphoto (Mixmike), Calgary, Alberta; (4) iStockphoto (Andyd), Calgary, Alberta; (5) iStockphoto (fotogal), Calgary, Alberta; (6) iStockphoto (LPETTET), Calgary, Alberta; S.18: (1) iStockphoto (dumayne), Calgary, Alberta; (2) iStockphoto (VFKA), Calgary, Alberta; S.19: (1) iStockphoto (Lugaaa), Calgary, Alberta; S.28: (1) Avenue Images GmbH (Corbis RF), Hamburg; (2) Alamy Images RM (Dennis MacDonald), Abingdon, Oxon; (3) Alamy Images RM (Jim West), Abingdon, Oxon; S.37: (1) DigitalVision, Maintal-Dörnigheim; S.38: (1) Fotosearch RF (PhotoDisc), Waukesha, WI; S.59: (1) Mauritius (Röder), Mittenwald; S.60: (1) Mauritius (Röder), Mittenwald; S.61: (1) Getty Images RF (Photo Disc), München; (2) iStockphoto (Harris Shiffman), Calgary, Alberta; (3) Getty Images RF (Photodisc), München; (4) Reiner Enkelmann, Filderstadt; (5) iStockphoto (RF/Nathan Watkins), Calgary, Alberta; S.63: (1) Klett-Archiv (Silberzahn), Stuttgart; S.69: (1) Klett-Archiv (Silberzahn), Stuttgart; (2) Klett-Archiv (Silberzahn), Stuttgart; S.73: (1) Picture-Alliance (epa AFI Kalnins), Frankfurt; S.74: (1) laif (Polaris), Köln; S.75: (1) Picture-Alliance (epa AFI Kalnins), Frankfurt; S. 87: Klett-Archiv; S.89: (1) Agence France-Presse GmbH, Berlin; S.92: (1) iStockphoto (RF/Jason Stitt), Calgary, Alberta; S.93: (1) Ingram Publishing, Tattenhall Chester; S.95: (1) MEV, Augsburg; (2) MEV, Augsburg; (3) MEV, Augsburg; S.101: (1) MEV, Augsburg; (2) Picture-Alliance (Picture Press/Camera), Frankfurt; (3) MEV, Augsburg; (4) Coca-Cola GmbH, Essen; (5) Helga Lade (K. Röhrig), Frankfurt; (6) MEV, Augsburg; S.102: (1) MEV, Augsburg; (2) Picture-Alliance (Picture Press/Camera), Frankfurt; (3) MEV, Augsburg; (4) Coca-Cola GmbH, Essen; (5) Siemens AG, München; (6) AKG, Berlin; (7) Helga Lade (K. Röhrig), Frankfurt; (8) MEV, Augsburg

© Ernst Klett Verlag GmbH, Stuttgart 2008 | www.klett.de
Von dieser Druckvorlage ist die Vervielfältigung für den eigenen Unterrichtsgebrauch gestattet. Die Kopiergebühren sind abgegolten. Alle Rechte vorbehalten.

Orange Line 4
ISBN 978-3-12-547544-1

103

Orange Line 4 Hörverstehenstexte zu den Standardaufgaben

Track	Unit	Übung	Seite	Text / Übungstitel	Spielzeit
1	GK 1	1	4	Let's listen: What's for lunch?	2'23"
2	GK 1	Zusatz		Let's listen: Interview with a New York window cleaner	2'25"
3	GK 2	1	20	Let's listen: The art of dating	1'50"
4	GK 2	Zusatz		Let's listen: Make a Difference Day	1'18"
5	GK 3	1	32	Let's listen: Problems in a hotel	2'24"
6	GK 3	Zusatz		Let's listen: Interview with a journalist	2'07"
7	GK 4	1	47	Let's listen: Our flight is delayed	2'32"
8	GK 4	Zusatz		Let's listen: Discussion about which vacation	2'23"
9	GK 5	1	62	Let's listen: Summer movies	2'13"
10	GK 5	Zusatz		Let's listen: A conversation about music	2'09"
11	EK 1	1	4	Let's listen: What's for lunch?	3'03"
12	EK 1	Zusatz		Let's listen: Interview with a New York window cleaner	3'50"
13	EK 2	1	20	Let's listen: The art of dating	2'30"
14	EK 2	Zusatz		Let's listen: Make a Difference Day	1'58"
15	EK 3	1	32	Let's listen: Problems in a hotel	2'24"
16	EK 3	Zusatz		Let's listen: Interview with a journalist	3'26"
17	EK 4	1	47	Let's listen: Our flight is delayed	3'41"
18	EK 4	Zusatz		Let's listen: Discussion about which vacation	3'16"
19	EK 5	1	62	Let's listen: Summer movies	2'55"
20	EK 5	Zusatz		Let's listen: A conversation about music	2'44"

Gesamtspielzeit: 51'41"

Lehrersoftware-CD

Empfohlene Systemvoraussetzungen:

- PC mit 500 MHz oder höher
- Windows 98 SE, ME, 2000, XP, Vista
- 128 MB RAM
- S-VGA-kompatible Grafikkarte mit 16,7 Mio Farben (24 bit)
- mind. 50 MB bis max. 450 MB freier Speicherplatz bei Kopie der Medien auf die Festplatte
- 24fach CD-ROM-Laufwerk
- Bildschirmauflösung (Programm) 800 x 600 Pixel
- Schwarzweiß- oder Farbdrucker mit 300 dpi Druckauflösung
- Microsoft Word (ab Version 2000) oder OpenOffice (ab Version 2.0)

Abspiel-Umgebungen und Datei-Betrachter für die Medien befinden sich auf der CD-ROM.

Schnellstart der Software:

Die Installation kopiert das Programm auf die Festplatte Ihres Rechners. Wir empfehlen, die Medien sofort auf der Festplatte zu installieren. Sie brauchen dann die CD-ROM nicht mehr einzulegen, um das Programm zu verwenden.

- Legen Sie die Lehrersoftware-CD in Ihr CD-ROM-Laufwerk ein.
- Die Autostartfunktion öffnet ein Fenster mit dem Inhalt der CD-ROM.
- Starten Sie die Datei „SETUP.EXE" durch Doppelklick und folgen Sie den Anweisungen, um das Programm und die Medien auf Ihrer Festplatte zu installieren.
- Um das Programm zu installieren, müssen Sie dem Lizenzvertrag zustimmen (s. a. **Lizenz.txt** auf der CD-ROM).
- Den Pfad für die Programminstallation auf der Festplatte können Sie anpassen oder nach der Vorgabe übernehmen.
- Sie starten das Programm über Ihr Startmenü (Start – Programme – Klett Lehrersoftware – Orange Line – Lehrersoftware Orange Line)

Auf der CD-ROM befindet sich ein ausführliches Handbuch zum Programm.

Orange Line 4
ISBN 978-3-12-547544-1
© Ernst Klett Verlag GmbH, Stuttgart 2008 | www.klett.de
Von dieser Druckvorlage ist die Vervielfältigung für den eigenen Unterrichtsgebrauch gestattet. Die Kopiergebühren sind abgegolten. Alle Rechte vorbehalten.